HEALTH	
FAMILY	
HOME	39
WORK & RETIREMENT	57
MONEY	73
TRAVEL & TRANSPORT	95
GOODS & SERVICES	113
LEISURE	125
SAFETY	143
THE LEGAL SYSTEM	155
GOVERNMENT	173
CONTACTS	185

In trying to summarise the law, we have had to leave out some details which might be relevant to your own situation, therefore do not use this book as proof of your legal rights. Before taking any legal action you should always take further advice. Often the best place to start is the Citizens Advice Bureau, but there are many others. Remember too that the law is always changing. To the best of our knowledge, we have described the law as it stood on 1 February 1998.

We would particularly like to thank Age Concern, the Citizen's Charter Unit, Guardian Insurance plc, Saga and the Law Society for their generous support of this project.

Age Concern cares about all older people and finds effective ways to make later life fulfilling and enjoyable.

The aim of the Charter Programme is to raise standards of public services and make them more responsive to their users.

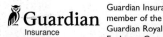

Guardian Insurance is a member of the Guardian Royal Exchange Group, a major international insurance group offering a full range of insurance and related financial services. For further information call 0171 283 7101.

Saga is the longest established provider of specialist holidays and financial services for people aged 50 and over. For further information you can call free on 0800 300 456, or write to Saga Holidays, The Saga Building, Middelburg Square, Folkestone, Kent CT20 1AZ.

SAGA

THE LAW SOCIETY

The Citizenship Foundation would like to thank the Law Society for their continued support with this and other projects.

Main author and editor Tony Thorpe

Concept devised by Andrew Phillips, Chairman of the Citizenship Foundation.

With thanks to Kathleen Bennett, Peter Bettley, Martyn Bond, Tim Bull, Robert Byk, Liba Cohen, Gloria Craig, Verity Danziger, Mary Domanska, Helen Driscoll, Rod Duckworth, Stuart Duggan, Steve Evans, Jeremy Fennell, Sarah Greenhaf, Michael Grimes, Alison Hook, Jo Lawrence, Liz Lawrence, Penny Letts, Dan Mace, Evelyn McEwen, Jan Newton, Jessica Newton, John Pearson, Penelope Phillips, John Robins, Richard Welfare, Crispin Rooney, Don Rowe, Sapna Shah, Dinah Tuck, Katie Vanstone, the staff of Doncaster Public Library and to the groups of older people we spoke to from Bromley, Doncaster, Evesham and Retford. Also to Andrew, Ella and Ray Pearson and the Galleries of Justice, Nottingham for the loan of objects for photography.

Photography by Lee Stanley,
Ulrike Preuss (Intro) and Simon Burt (page 164). *Other photographs kindly reproduced with permission from* © Age Concern England: pages Intro, 3, 7, 28, 29, 47, 53, 58, 60, 70, 72, 82, 88, 112, 130, 151, 173;
© Age Concern Swindon: page 84;
© Shirley A Hedger/Age Concern: page 12;
© Campbell McCallum/Age Concern: page 128;
© Adrian Spalding/Age Concern: Intro;
John-Paul Stankowski/Age Concern: page 61;
© UNESCO/E Kosuthova/Age Concern: page 21;
by courtesy of Boys' Magazine: page 161;
by courtesy of the First Garden City Heritage Museum: pages 18, 44, 57, 62, 63, 64, 69, 70, 77, 78, 85, 96, 98, 120, 130, 180, 181;
by courtesy of the Liverpool Daily Post & Echo plc: page 153; by courtesy of Titbits: page 147; by courtesy of the Yorkshire Post: page 112; Kent Messenger Group Newspapers: page 76;
© Metropolitan Police: pages 108, 148, 150, 157, 159, 166.

Designed and illustrated by Nomad Graphique: Mike Gibas, Lena Lo, Rupert Boddington, John Dean and Laura Emms.

Cataloguing in Publication Data is available from The British Library

ISBN 0 340 711884

First published 1998

Impression number 10 9 8 7 6 5 4 3 2 1
Year 2001 2000 1999 1998

Printed in Great Britain for Hodder & Stoughton Educational, a division of Hodder Headline Plc, 338 Euston Road, London NW1 3BH by Bath Press

HEALTH

NATIONAL HEALTH SERVICE

CONSENT TO TREATMENT

MENTAL HEALTH ·

ACCESS TO RECORDS

COMPLAINTS

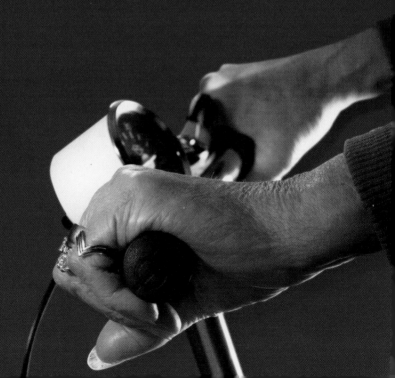

THE NATIONAL HEALTH SERVICE

In the early 1990s, the NHS was extensively reorganised under a system of contracts between purchasers and providers of health care.

From 1999, this is likely to change. Each Health Authority will be required to draw up a three year *Health Improvement Programme* for the local community - in consultation with GPs, community nurses, social services and NHS Trusts. The Health Authority will allocate money to what will be known as *Primary Care Groups* (local GPs and community nurses), which will decide how to deploy these resources to achieve the targets set in the Health Authority's Health Improvement Programme.

The words they use

Community Health Councils	Local independent committees, set up to represent the interests of patients in the community. They offer advice and practical help to anyone dissatisfied with their treatment by part of the NHS. See under "C" in the 'phone book for your local Community Health Council.
Family Health Services	A general term covering GPs, dentists, opticians, and pharmacists.
GPs	Short for general practitioners. Local doctors normally working from a surgery or health centre.
GP Fundholders	GPs who have control of their budget and buy some services for their patients direct from hospitals. For non-GP Fundholders, these services are provided by the local Health Authority. Under the proposed changes, GP Fundholders are likely to disappear.
Health Authorities	Responsible for assessing the health needs in their area and for obtaining the services to meet these needs. If you need to contact your Health Authority, your local GP surgery or health centre will be able to give you the number.
Health Improvement Programme	A local strategy or plan for improving health care.
NHS Trusts	The main providers of NHS services. Almost all hospitals and hospital services are run by Trusts.
Primary Care Groups	If the Government's proposals go ahead, these will comprise all the GPs and community nurses within an area, who will have the responsibility for organising health services for the local community.

GENERAL PRACTITIONERS

Everyone resident in the United Kingdom, including visitors from overseas, is entitled to register with a GP. A list of local GPs is available from your local Health Authority, Community Health Council, main post office, library and Citizens Advice Bureau.

You may change your GP at any time. There is no need to inform your doctor of your decision to change, or to explain why you are taking such action. If you move outside the practice area, but wish to keep your present GP, it's up to her or him to decide whether to allow you to stay on the practice list.

If you need help in deciding which GP to choose, all practices should have leaflets with the names, ages and qualifications of the doctors who work in there, the surgery times, arrangements for home visits and off duty cover, and the area covered by the practice. New patients are entitled to a health examination when they join a practice.

GPs can refuse to accept a new patient, and need not give a reason for their decision.

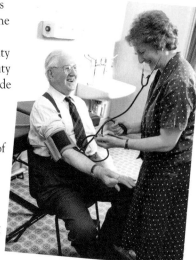

However, if this does occur, the Health Authority has a duty to provide the patient with details of local GPs within two working days.

If you are staying, for up to three months, in another part of the United Kingdom you can ask to be registered with another GP on a temporary basis. The GP will need to see your medical card or know your National Health number. If you have lost your medical card, a replacement can be obtained free of charge from your local Health Authority.

All patients aged 75 or over should be offered a health check on a yearly basis - although they don't have to accept it. The examination can take place either at the surgery or at home - whichever the patient prefers.

Patients are normally expected to consult their doctor during surgery hours. However, doctors do have a duty to make home visits or to arrange for the patient to be seen by another doctor or admitted to hospital, if the patient's condition requires it. There may be grounds for complaint if a doctor fails to do this and the patient suffers as a result.

A doctor does not have to agree to a patient's request for a second opinion. However, if the GP is in doubt about the diagnosis and fails to refer the patient to a specialist, and the patient suffers as a result, the patient may again have cause for complaint on grounds of negligence. For more information on the complaints procedure, see pages 17 - 20.

CHARGES AND PRESCRIPTIONS

There are no charges for GP care and treat-ment in the NHS - although a doctor may charge a temporary patient who is unable to produce his or her medical card or National Health number. This happens very rarely, and if it does, the patient is able to reclaim the money from their own Health

Authority when they return home.

GPs are, however, allowed to charge for certain other services, such as holiday vaccinations, sickness certificates and medical examinations for insurance purposes.

Free prescriptions are available to anyone aged 60 or over, anyone who receives (or whose partner receives) Income Support, income-based Jobseeker's Allowance, Family Credit or Disability Working Allowance, or anyone whose name is on a current HC2 charges certificate. Free prescriptions are also available to people suffering from certain medical conditions. Further details are available from GPs, post offices, social security offices, the Citizens Advice Bureau and booklet HC11, *Are you entitled to help with health costs?*

DENTISTS

NHS dentists now operate what is called a *continuing care* programme, requiring patients to attend for a checkup or treatment at least once every 15 months. Patients who do not maintain contact with their dentist over this period risk losing their entitlement to NHS care with that dentist. Once a dentist accepts a patient for continuing care, the patient must be provided, on the NHS, with all the treatment

necessary for dental health.

Before each course of treatment, the patient will receive a treatment plan, showing the work the dentist intends to carry out and what it will cost. A dentist may offer to treat a patient privately, but should not place pressure on the patient by implying that the treatment is not available on the NHS. A patient is under no obligation to accept the treatment being offered.

If you wish to change dentists - and you may do so at any time - your local Community Health Council, Health Authority and Citizens Advice Bureau can provide you with a list of NHS dentists. The Health Authority should, within five working days, be able to find you a dentist who can give you NHS treatment.

If you need emergency treatment but are not registered for continuing care, you should contact a local NHS dentist to see if he or she is prepared to accept you on an emergency basis. If they are unable to see you, contact your local Health Authority, who should be able to find a dentist prepared to provide treatment.

Most dental treatment is subject to charges. Free treatment is available to anyone who receives (or whose partner receives) Income Support, income-based Jobseeker's Allowance, Family Credit or Disability Working Allowance and anyone whose name is on a current HC2 charges certificate. A person who does not qualify for free dental treatment, or help with the cost, must pay up to 80% of the cost up to a maximum of £340 (April 1998).

There is no *extra* fee for emergency treatment. Nor is there a charge for an emergency call-out or home visit. A patient registered with a dentist for continuing care must be visited at home if their condition makes it impossible for them to attend the surgery - provided they live within five miles of the surgery.

A dentist may charge a patient who fails to keep an appointment or cancels at very short notice. The level of charge varies from one dentist to another.

Anyone with a disability which makes it difficult for them to receive dental care can be put in touch with a dentist with experience of working with disabled people through either the Community Dental Service or the British Society of Dentistry for the Handicapped. See **Contacts** for details.

OBTAINING HEALTH CARE

OPTICIANS

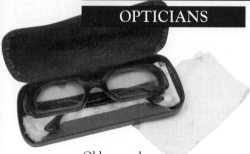

Older people are not entitled to free annual sight tests, although some opticians do offer reduced rates to people of state pension age.

Among others who qualify for free NHS sight tests are those who receive (or whose partner receives) Income Support, income-based Jobseeker's Allowance, Family Credit or Disability Working Allowance and anyone whose name is on a current HC2 charges certificate. Free sight tests are also available for someone who is registered blind or partially sighted, who needs complex lenses or who suffers from certain medical conditions. Further information is available from opticians, the Citizens Advice Bureau and booklet HC11, *Are you entitled to help with health costs?*

Spectacles are no longer available on the NHS. But help towards the cost of glasses or contact lenses is available to people listed above.

If you find it difficult to visit an optician, some will offer home visits. They are not obliged to do this, and there may be a charge. In some areas there are visiting schemes in which opticians participate on a voluntary basis. Alternatively, help may be available through a health visitor, district nurse or the local hospital.

CHIROPODISTS

Unlike most other services, NHS chiropody care is available only to certain priority groups, including women over 60 and men over 65. Many people opt to be treated privately.

THE HEALTH INFORMATION SERVICE

A free confidential service, operating 9.30am - 5.00pm Monday - Friday. It can provide information on a wide variety of health matters, including health care and treatment in your area and what to do if you are not happy with the treatment or service you have been given, tel 0800 66 55 44.

HOSPITALS
Waiting lists

The *Patient's Charter* guarantees that, whatever medical condition a patient is suffering from, she or he should not have to wait more than 18 months for admission to hospital for treatment. For some illnesses, the waiting period should be much shorter, and many Health Authorities have set their own waiting standards, which improve on this. Patients admitted for an accident or emergency should be seen and assessed for treatment immediately.

The *Charter* also states that operations should not be cancelled on the day a patient is due to go into hospital or after they have been admitted. If an operation is cancelled, the patient can expect to be given a new date for the operation which will be within one month of the cancellation.

There is a National Waiting List Helpline for England and Wales, to help members of the public find out which hospitals have shorter waiting lists. This is operated by the College of Health, tel 0181 983 1133.

Treatment

There is no absolute right for patients to choose either the hospital at which they will be treated or the consultant responsible for their care. The consultant may delegate the task of examining the patient to another doctor in his or her team, but the consultant retains overall responsibility for the patient. A patient cannot insist on a particular treatment if the doctor feels it is inappropriate.

There is no automatic right to a single sex ward, but patients should be informed of this before going into hospital, unless they are admitted as an emergency. Patients have the right to be examined and treated without medical students present if they wish.

Under the *Road Traffic Act 1988*, NHS hospitals and GPs are allowed to charge a fee for emergency treatment following a road accident. The charges are imposed on the users of the vehicles involved in the accident and are usually paid by their insurance companies.

CONSENT

Generally speaking, adults who are able to make their own decisions should not be examined or treated without their consent. Nor is it permissible for someone else to authorise examination or treatment on their behalf. However, an adult who cannot make or convey a decision will not be denied essential treatment. In such circumstances doctors may treat a patient according to what they believe are in his or her best interests. In some situations, for example before major surgery, it is thought wise to refer the decision to a court.

In order for consent to be valid,

the patient must understand the nature and purpose of the treatment, the possible alternatives and any substantial risks in order to make a balanced, informed judgment.

If, for example, during an operation, the need for other treatment becomes necessary, doctors must obtain fresh consent, unless the condition is life-threatening and requires immediate action. In this situation, the doctor would act in the patient's best interest and go ahead with the treatment - unless the patient had refused, in advance.

Difficulties clearly arise when the patient is unable either to communicate or to understand the consequences of accepting or rejecting the treatment being considered.

In deciding on the best course of action, the doctor should try to find out what the patient would have chosen had he or she been well enough to decide. This means taking account of any wishes the patient had previously expressed and talking to carers, close relatives and friends. However, this is not the same as asking carers or the next of kin to make a decision about the treatment, *on behalf of* the

In 1993, doctors wished to operate on a patient with a severe mental disorder who was suffering from a life threatening condition. The patient said that he did not wish to have the operation and applied to the court for an injunction to prevent the authorities from taking action. The court decided that, despite his mental condition, the patient understood the nature, purpose and effects of the proposed treatment and was therefore quite justified in refusing to have the operation.

patient. Next of kin have no legal right either to consent to or refuse treatment on the patient's behalf.

Advance directives

An advance directive (sometimes known as a *living will*) is a statement made by someone who is in a rational and lucid state about how they would like to be treated if they ever lose the capacity to make or convey a decision. An advance directive is as legally binding on the doctor as a refusal at the time would be - as long as it is validly made and applicable in the circumstances. An advance directive cannot authorise a doctor to do anything against the law.

The law states that it is unlawful for a doctor to administer treatment which is intended to cause death, even though the doctor may genuinely believe that the patient wishes to die. Therefore, any document written by a patient requesting this, would be invalid. However the courts have decided that it is

acceptable, in certain circumstances, to administer treatment which eases a patient's suffering even though that treatment might hasten an otherwise inevitable death. They have also decided that

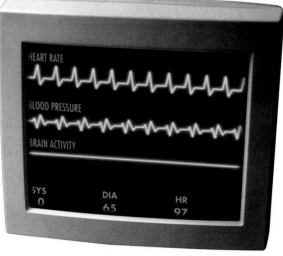

withdrawing or withholding life-saving treatment is also not inevitably a criminal act. The reasoning behind this is that, in such circumstances, the cause of death is the underlying illness and not, for example, the removal of the life-support machine. Further information on this subject is available from the Patient's Association and the Terrence Higgins Trust. See **Contacts** for details.

Research

In general, any research which involves a patient personally, requires his or her consent. A full explanation of the procedure and risks must be given. A patient can withdraw their consent at any time. No one can consent to research being carried out on another person.

LEAVING HOSPITAL

Before a patient is discharged from hospital, an assessment should be made of their continuing health and social care needs and whether there are any implications for their housing. A patient should not be discharged until it is clinically appropriate and until any necessary further arrangements have been made. The hospital should take account of the wishes of the patient, their family and carers, and should provide written details of community care services that will be provided.

If the support you are given is insufficient or unsatisfactory, contact the hospital or local social services department as soon as possible. Your local Community Health Council will also be able to help in these circumstances.

If a person is told that they will be discharged from hospital when they do not yet feel ready to leave or are not satisfied with the care arrangements proposed, the hospital, local social services and community care

© Shirley A. Hedger/Age Concern

staff will normally work with the patient, their family and carer to find a satisfactory alternative. If the problem cannot be resolved, however, the patient, their family or carer may ask the Health Authority to review the decision not to provide continuing NHS care.

The review panel comprises an independent chair and a representative from the Health Authority and the local authorities. It should be convened quickly, although patients do not have the right to insist that the review is undertaken.

However, if it does go ahead, it should be completed as a matter of urgency and should aim to provide the patient with a written reply within two weeks of their request. During this time, the patient should not be discharged from NHS care. The purpose of the panel is to check that the Health Authority's criteria for continuing in-patient care have been correctly applied. The review is not meant to be a process whereby the criteria themselves can be challenged.

MENTAL HEALTH CARE

Most people who receive hospital treatment for a mental illness are there through choice or because they have taken the advice of a doctor, psychiatrist or social worker. They are known, in law, as *informal* patients. In a relatively small number of cases, a person will refuse to be examined or treated and it may be decided that they should be admitted to hospital *compulsorily* under the *Mental Health Act 1983* (or sectioned, as it is often called), for assessment and treatment, in the interests of their own health or safety or for the protection of others.

An application for compulsory detention is normally made by a social worker, supported (except in an emergency) in writing by two doctors. One of the doctors must know the patient personally, and the other must have experience in the treatment of mental illness. An application for compulsory detention can also be made by the patient's nearest relative. When an application is made by a social worker, the nearest relative must also be consulted.

The circumstances under which a person may be detained for assessment or treatment are set out in the *Mental Health Act 1983*.

OBTAINING HEALTH CARE

A patient can be compulsorily detained for *assessment* for up to 28 days on the recommendation of two doctors. A person held for *treatment* can be kept in hospital for up to six months. Again two medical recommendations are required. Compulsory detention can be renewed for a further six months and then annually on the recommendation of the patient's doctor.

In an emergency, a person can be admitted to hospital for up to 72 hours on the application of a relative or social worker, supported by a doctor. The police also have emergency powers to remove someone who is in a public place and appears to be mentally ill and in need of immediate care.

This would usually be to a place of safety (ie a hospital) for up to 72 hours.

As an alternative to sectioning, a mentally ill patient may be placed in the care of a guardian (often the local social services), who will look after the person's interests and make sure that he or she receives the necessary care. The use of this procedure varies from one part of the country to another and is designed for people who do not need to be cared for in a hospital setting.

Voluntary patients may leave hospital whenever they wish, unless a doctor feels that this is inadvisable and applies for a detention order. The procedure for the release of patients detained compulsorily is more complex. Further, and more detailed, information on this is available from your local regional office of the mental health charity, MIND. Your local Community Health Council and the Health Information Service will be able to provide you with the address and telephone number. Copies of the *Patient's Charter: Mental Health Services* and other information on mental illness are also available from the Health Information Service, tel 0800 66 55 44.

ACCESS TO RECORDS

You have a right, under the *Data Protection Act 1984* to see or obtain a copy of the information held on computer about you, with an explanation of terms that are not clear. A fee of up to £10 may be charged. If you find that the records contain information which is incorrect or misleading, you are entitled to apply to have it altered or removed.

The *Access to Health Records Act 1990* extends right of access to include manual health records produced after 1st November 1991 and, like the *Data Protection Act*, applies to both NHS and private health records. Anyone wishing to see their records should write to the person or organisation holding the records. No reason need be given for the request. Access includes a right to see and have copies of the original records and to have an explanation of the terminology used. A fee of no more than £10 may be charged, in addition to the cost of any photocopies.

For records produced before 1991, the *Code of Practice on Openness in the NHS* commits health authorities, trusts, doctors and other practitioners to release information to patients, on request.

However, this is not quite the same as providing actual copies of the files themselves. But it is the view of the *Health Service Ombudsman* (see page 19) that, provided none of the information being asked for is exempt, photocopies of the original should be provided.

It is also possible, under the *Access to Health Records Act*, for a patient to give someone else the authority to inspect their records, but permission must be given in writing.

The *personal representative* (see page 36) of someone who has died has a right to see that person's health records, unless the deceased left instructions forbidding that person access. However, a doctor should not release information supplied in confidence by the deceased in the expectation that the doctor would continue to respect that confidence after the patient's death.

MEDICAL RECORDS
PRIVATE AND CONFIDENTIAL
FOR INTERNAL USE ONLY
(CANCEL PREVIOUS ADDRESS)

PLEASE USE REVERSE

CITIZENSHIP
FOUNDATION

OBTAINING HEALTH CARE

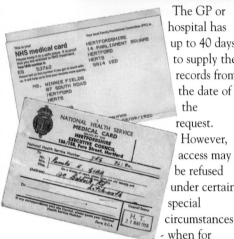

The GP or hospital has up to 40 days to supply the records from the date of the request. However, access may be refused under certain special circumstances - when for example, it is felt access is likely to cause serious harm to the patient's mental or physical wellbeing. There is no general right of access to records which were created before November 1991, although it is possible for a patient who is preparing a case and bringing legal proceedings against a doctor or hospital to see or obtain copies of their records with the permission of the court.

If you believe your records contain an error, you may ask for the record to be amended. If the holder of the record is unwilling to do this, you may apply to a court and your concern about their accuracy must be recorded.

If a *Freedom of Information Act* comes into force, as the Government plans, public access to medical information is likely to improve. However the law is unlikely to reach the statute book before the years 1999 or 2000.

Medical reports for insurance and employment

Under the *Access to Medical Reports Act 1988*, an employer or insurance company may not apply to your doctor for a medical report about you without first notifying you and informing you of your rights under the Act. You have a right to see the report before it is sent and no charge may be made for this. If you want a photocopy of the report, then the charge must be reasonable. If you believe the report is inaccurate or misleading you can ask the doctor to amend it. If he or she refuses, you can ask for a statement of your views to be attached to the report. The doctor should keep a copy of the report for up to six months after sending it, and you have the right to look at it again during this period.

COMPLAINTS PROCEDURE

The *Patient's Charter* (to be replaced by a new *NHS Charter* by 1999) sets out the rights and standard of service that patients can expect to receive from all parts of the NHS. It also indicates the steps you can take if you wish to make a complaint about the treatment or service you have received.

If you have a complaint, it is important that it should be made as soon as possible. Generally, six months is allowed from the date of the incident or the discovery of the problem, as long as it is within twelve months of the initial event. Complaints are normally made by the person concerned, but they can be put forward by someone else, as long as the patient agrees to action being taken on their behalf.

Legal aid is not available to people going through the complaints procedure, although some initial legal advice may be provided by a solicitor free, or at a reduced rate, under the *legal advice and assistance scheme*. See page 170 for further details.

Help is also available from the local Community Health Council, which can provide information and advice about all aspects of the complaints procedure and is sometimes able to conduct a complaint on a patient's behalf.

The NHS complaints procedure is in two stages, **Local resolution** and **Independent Review**. Before presenting a complaint it's important to think about the kind of outcome that you require. Do you wish to register dissatisfaction and receive an apology or, perhaps, to try to ensure that something similar does not happen again? If you are considering bringing legal proceedings, it is important to know that the NHS complaints procedure will cease as soon as it is clear that legal action is being contemplated.

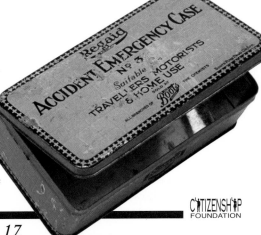

MAKING A COMPLAINT

LOCAL RESOLUTION
Family Health Services

Many GPs, dentists, opticians etc. have leaflets explaining the procedure to follow if you have a complaint about the service you have received. If you would rather not complain direct, contact the complaints

NOEL HOME

manager at your Health Authority who may be able to advise you or pass on your concerns to the person in question.

If your complaint cannot be dealt with straightaway, it should be referred to the practice complaints manager. Under the *Patient's Charter*, you should receive an acknowledgment of your call or letter within two working days and a full response within ten. You should be informed if it is likely to take longer than this to deal with your case.

Hospital services

If you have a complaint, it is usually best to start by bringing it to the attention of the person or section of the hospital you feel is responsible. If this is not appropriate, or you wish to take it further, then write to the Trust or hospital complaints manager. Under the *Patient's Charter*, you should expect an acknowledgment and then a full reply from the chief executive or general manager within four weeks.

INDEPENDENT REVIEW

If you are dissatisfied with the response you receive at the local resolution stage and wish to take the matter further, you can ask the Health Authority or hospital Trust for an independent review. A request of this kind should be made within four weeks of the date of the letter telling you the outcome of the local resolution.

There is, however, no guarantee that an independent review will be granted. Your request will be passed to someone, called a convenor, who will examine your complaint and choose one of a number of options. These include asking for further action to be taken under local resolution,

HEALTH

MAKING A COMPLAINT

proposing that both sides attend a conciliation meeting, setting up the independent review panel or recommending that no further action be taken.

If a review is undertaken, it will be carried out by three people who will speak to everyone involved in a relatively informal way and probably not in the form of a court. The panel will give its findings and recommendations in a report, but these cannot include proposals about disciplinary matters. It is up to the Health Authority or Trust to decide what further action should be taken.

If you still remain unhappy with the outcome, you may wish to report the matter to the *Health Service Ombudsman* or take the case to the professional body of the person concerned, eg. the General Medical Council. If the complaint relates to the detention of someone under the Mental Health Act, you should refer the complaint to the *Mental Health Act Commission*. See **Contacts**.

HEALTH SERVICE OMBUDSMAN

A case can be referred to the Ombudsman only after the complaints procedure has been exhausted and no later than a year from the date when you became aware of the issue about which you are concerned. Sometimes, if there are special reasons, the Ombudsman can extend this time limit.

You will need to give full details of your complaint in writing with copies of all correspondence that you have received. A leaflet on this, with a complaints form, is available from main libraries, the Citizens Advice Bureau and the Office of the Health Service Ombudsman, see **Contacts** for details. Help will also be available from your local Community Health Council and Member of Parliament.

PRIVATE PATIENTS

Private hospitals, unlike the NHS, are not required to have a complaints procedure, although some do. However, private patients have a contract with the hospital or doctor who is treating them and, as a result, may take legal action for breach of contract if they are dissatisfied with the treatment received. But this is not a step to be taken lightly and it is important to take legal advice from a solicitor with experience in these matters.

JUDICIAL REVIEW

Someone who wishes to challenge a decision made by a hospital, health or local authority may apply for a judicial review. If the challenge is successful, the court can declare that the public body's decision was unlawful and quash it, forcing the matter to be reconsidered, using the correct procedure or interpretation of the law.

Generally, the courts require applications for judicial review to be made within three months of the date of the decision that is being questioned. This is not a simple area of law and so, before doing anything, it is important to obtain advice from a solicitor with some experience of working in this area. See page 184 for further details.

LEGAL ACTION

If you believe the treatment you received was negligent and caused you suffering or damage, you may wish to look into the possibility of bringing legal proceedings for negligence against the doctor

or Trust concerned.

In order to succeed in an action for medical negligence, you must be able to show that the care you received fell *well* below the standard that can reasonably be expected. It's also necessary to show that the negligence caused the injury from which you are suffering. If there is any doubt that the injury was caused by the doctor's or hospital's negligence or it is decided that negligence occurred without causing injury, then no damages will be recoverable.

Action of this kind is usually costly and complex. It is possible to get legal aid to fund such a claim but, before taking any action, it is very important to obtain advice from a solicitor with experience in these matters. Action for Victims of Medical Accidents (AVMA) and the Law Society can help you find a lawyer experienced in this field. See **Contacts** for details.

Generally, patients have three years from the date of injury to bring an action.

FAMILY

MARRIAGE

LIVING TOGETHER

SEPARATION & DIVORCE

DEATH

FUNERALS & WILLS

MARRIAGE

For a marriage to be legally valid it must be between two people who want to marry and are
• over the age of 16,
• of the opposite sex,
• not already married, and
• not closely related.

A man cannot marry his mother (or adoptive mother), sister, daughter (or adoptive daughter), granddaughter, aunt or niece. But he can, with some restrictions, marry his step-mother, step-daughter, step-granddaughter or mother-in-law. For example, a man can marry his step-daughter if she has not been brought up by him as a child of the family and he may only marry his daughter-in-law if they are both over 21 and both his son and wife are dead. The same rules apply to a woman in respect of her male relations.

Being married to more than one person at the same time - bigamy - is normally a crime.

You Are Invited...

...To Our Wedding!

But polygamous marriage is recognised in England and Wales if it took place in a country which allows polygamy and neither partner was living in England or Wales at the time of marriage.

Consequences

Marriage has certain financial and legal implications. A person's tax position may change, as may their entitlement to state benefits and community care services. For a widow, it may result in the loss of the pension provided through her late husband's employment or her state widow's pension. Marriage also revokes a person's will - in its entirety. If one of the partners dies before a new will is drawn up, the person is said to have died *intestate*, and the bulk of the estate may pass to the new spouse. It is therefore important for both partners to make a new will before or shortly after the marriage. For more information, see pages 34-38.

MARRIAGE

ENGAGEMENT

Until the law was changed in 1970, an engagement was seen as a legal agreement or contract between two people to marry. If it was broken, one person could sue the other for damages. Today this does not apply and there is usually no legal duty even to return the ring. An engagement ring is seen as a gift, and may be kept unless it was originally agreed to return it if the marriage did not take place.

Other gifts, however, are given on the assumption that the wedding will take place. If it falls through, wedding guests are entitled to the return of their gifts.

THE MARRIAGE CEREMONY

Unless you are divorced and your spouse is still alive, you can be married in an Anglican church, even if you are neither a churchgoer nor believer, as long as you satisfy the

legal requirements and qualify as a resident of the parish.

Members of other faiths and denominations (e.g. Sikh, Muslim, Baptist, Roman Catholic) must first obtain a civil certificate or licence from the senior registrar of the district where they live. The marriage ceremony may then take place in a registered building or chapel. For Jewish and Quaker weddings, different rules apply and the ceremony need not take place in a registered building.

Until the *Marriage Act 1994*, couples could only marry in the register office of the district in which they lived. Now they can choose to marry in any registry office in England and Wales. Local authorities can also approve other premises, such as hotels and stately homes. The room in which the ceremony takes place must be suitable for the occasion and not a temporary structure, such as a marquee or the open air.

CHANGE OF NAME

Many women in Britain change their surname when they marry - they don't *have* to do this. A woman can keep her own family name, or she can make a new one by joining her name with that of her husband.

CITIZENSHIP FOUNDATION

LIVING TOGETHER

An increasing number of couples live together, sometimes with the thought of marrying later and, sometimes not. Although a matter of personal choice, the law treats married and unmarried couples very differently.

MONEY AND FINANCE

Couples who *marry* have a legal duty to look after one another, and to provide each other with financial support - which may continue even if the marriage ends in divorce. But a couple who *live together* without getting married, are under no such duty, unless it is something they have specifically agreed to do.

Couples who *marry* have an extra tax allowance, which means that they usually pay less tax than if they were just living together. A couple *living together* may be subject to capital gains tax on certain gifts to each other and to inheritance tax in the event of the death of one of the partners. This does not apply between people who are *married*.

Pension and benefit rights are often better for a *married* than an unmarried woman, particularly when her partner dies. However a widow who remarries may lose her entitlement to a private pension from her late husband's work. This is unlikely to happen if she lives with someone.

If a married person dies without making a will, their partner is entitled to all or most of their estate. If they were not married, it can be very difficult for the other to have any of his or her partner's possessions, unless the deceased left a valid will. (For further information, see page 36.)

HOME

A *married* couple have equal rights to occupy their home, whether they rent or own it - and this continues even if their marriage fails, unless the court orders otherwise.

When an *unmarried* couple live together, the non-owner of the home normally has no right to occupy the property, nor has any interest in the property. However, if the couple have lived together for some time, the non-owning partner may have acquired some rights to the property under law. Couples can avoid difficulties caused by this by using a solicitor to write a formal contract which sets out what would happen to their house and contents etc. should the relationship come to an end.

SEPARATION & DIVORCE

Married couples no longer wishing to live together face the decision of separating or ending their marriage by divorce.

SEPARATION

Arrangements for separation can range from an informal agreement to a court decree of judicial separation. For couples who separate informally there may be no need to take any kind of legal action at all. However there may still be obligations to look after the children and the other partner. If the couple do eventually seek a divorce, arrangements made during this intervening period may affect the decision of a court.

Some couples in this position seek legal advice and draw up a *separation agreement*, which is a statement, written by the couple, indicating how they propose to deal with questions relating to their children, money and property. It is wise for both partners to take legal advice over this.

Separation changes the benefits position of many people. Further information is available from Social Security offices and Benefits Agency leaflets, available from the Citizens Advice Bureau, libraries and post offices.

Judicial separation

A couple who do not want to divorce, but still wish their separation to be legally recognised, may apply for a decree of judicial separation. This does not dissolve the marriage, or leave the partners free to remarry, but does release them from their duty to live together. A decree may be granted, unlike a divorce, within the first year of a couple's marriage and the grounds for judicial separation are the same as those for a divorce (see below). The financial arrangements of couples granted a judicial separation are dealt with in a similar way had they been divorced.

Under the *Family Law Act 1996*, separation orders will replace decrees of judicial separation - but this is not likely to come into force until 1999.

C*TIZENSH*P
FOUNDATION

SEPARATION & DIVORCE

DIVORCE

Major changes in the divorce law will take place when the *Family Law Act 1996* comes into effect - probably in 1999. Until then, the existing law applies, based on the *Matrimonial Causes Act 1973*.

Grounds for divorce

Under the present law, someone applying for a divorce, must prove to the court that their marriage has irretrievably broken down. Any *one* of the following situations is accepted as evidence of this....

• that one partner has committed adultery and the other finds it intolerable to continue living with them;

• that one partner has behaved unreasonably. This covers many things, including assault and being excessively dirty or unsociable;

• that they have lived apart for two years, and they both want a divorce;

• that they have lived apart for five years and only one partner wants a divorce; or

• that one partner has deserted the other for at least two years.

Couples are unable to obtain a divorce in the first year of their marriage.

Procedure

When one or both partners decide to divorce, an application is made, usually through a solicitor, to the local county court or the Divorce Registry. The solicitor will ask about the possibility of reconciliation and will be able to suggest ways in which guidance or counselling can be obtained, if it is thought this would be helpful. If there is no chance of repairing the marriage, the application for the divorce will continue, although it is possible for the couple to stop the proceedings at any time until the award of the decree absolute.

If the couple can agree over their finances and make satisfactory plans for the care of their children under the age of 17, it will probably not be necessary for either to appear in court. Nor will there be any publicity in the papers, unless the divorce is defended or reporting restrictions are lifted. If the District Judge is satisfied that the appropriate arrangements have been made and that the marriage has irretrievably broken down, he or she will grant a *decree nisi*, which is the first stage in granting a divorce. Six weeks and one day later, the person seeking the divorce can apply for a *decree absolute* and, when this is granted, the marriage comes to an end.

SEPARATION & DIVORCE

Changes to the law

When the *Family Law Act 1996* comes into force, there will then be only one ground for divorce - that the marriage has irretrievably broken down. There will be no need, as there is now, to give evidence of adultery, unreasonable behaviour, desertion or that the couple have lived apart for two or five years.

The new procedure will work in the following way. First the couple will attend an informal meeting (either separately or together), where they will be given information on counselling, mediation and the divorce process. A period of at least three months must then elapse. If one or both partners still wishes to apply for a divorce, they submit a formal statement to the court, explaining why the marriage has broken down and cannot be saved.

A compulsory period of reflection and consideration follows this - lasting for 18 months if the couple still have children under 16, or for nine months, if they do not. If, at the end of this period, either or both partners still wish to go ahead with the divorce, the marriage will be formally ended with a divorce order, provided the court is satisfied with the arrangements that have been made for any children and the couple's finances.

Violence

A court can make an order or injunction to protect a victim of domestic violence and can order one partner to leave the home for the other's protection. The range of relationships covered by the law has recently been widened. Under the *Family Law Act 1996*, protection is available to an elderly person who is being abused by another family member. It is important for anyone in this situation to get advice from a solicitor as soon as possible.

CITIZENSHIP
FOUNDATION

SEPARATION & DIVORCE

Children

Parents going through a divorce are encouraged to try to reach agreement between themselves over all issues, including where their children will live and how often they will see each parent. The judge will accept these arrangements only if satisfied that they are in the best interests of the child. If the child is thought to be old enough to have a view, he or she will be consulted by the judge in private.

Parents who cannot agree over this are advised not to go straight to court (expensive and stressful for all concerned), but to negotiate through solicitors or use independent counsellors and mediation to help them sort out their problems. A court will, however, have to approve the final arrangements over children and money. It's usually felt to be in the children's interest to keep in touch with their family, so a judge will rarely stop a parent from seeing a child.

After the divorce, both parents normally keep parental responsibility for their child, and both should consult each other over decisions which affect their child's life, such as education, medical treatment and religious upbringing.

GRANDPARENTS

Grandparents can play an important role in their grandchildren's lives, especially if the relationship between the parents breaks down. Under the *Children Act 1989*, they are entitled to apply for a variety of rights in relation to their grandchildren. These include what are known as *Section 8 orders*, covering such matters as where the child will live, whom she or he will see, his or her education, medical treatment or removal from the country.

Grandparents first need the permission of the court to apply for such orders, unless they already have the consent of the parents (or whoever else has parental responsibility), or unless their grandchild has lived with them for at least three years. This need not have been for a continuous period, but must not have begun more than five years before.

In most cases, grandparents will seek a *contact order* - and the court will base its decision on what it feels is in the best interest of the child. *Residence orders* are more difficult for grandparents to obtain as courts tend to feel that, whenever possible, it is in the child's interest to stay with her or his natural parents.

When a child is taken into care, the local authority, under the *Children Act 1989*, is encouraged to make sure that grandparents

continue to be involved in the child's life and that they are consulted over important decisions concerning the child's welfare. Grandparents dissatisfied with the arrangements may apply to the court for a *contact order*, as above.

Adoption

When a child is adopted, all legal ties with the grandparents are broken - although, in exceptional circumstances, courts have decided to allow grandparents contact with a child if it is thought to be in that child's best interest.

CITIZENSHIP
FOUNDATION

DEATH

IMMEDIATE ISSUES

If the cause of death is quite clear, a doctor will complete a *Medical Certificate* certifying that death has occurred and giving the cause. The doctor will also give the next of kin a *Formal Notice*, stating that the doctor has signed the Medical Certificate and explaining how to register the death.

If the exact cause of death is unknown, the doctor will not be able to sign the certificate, but will contact the coroner who will decide whether a postmortem or an inquest is necessary. The coroner must also be informed if the death has occurred due to an industrial disease, under anaesthetic or during an operation, in suspicious circumstances, in prison or police custody, or if the person had not been seen by the doctor looking after them either during the 14 days prior to death or after death.

If a postmortem takes place and shows the cause of death to be due to natural causes, the coroner will issue *Form 100B* to the next of kin or registrar so the death can be registered.

If the death was not due to natural causes, the coroner will hold an *inquest*. This will be in public and possibly with a jury. The purpose of the inquest is to determine when, where and how the death occurred. Anyone with a proper interest in the case may question a witness about the medical evidence or other events surrounding the death.

A *Certificate for Cremation* or *Order for Burial* will be issued by the coroner either during or after the inquest, so that the death can be registered and arrangements made for the funeral.

Organ donation and medical research

If the person who died wished to have their body used for medical purposes, it is important to inform a doctor as soon as possible - as some organs may be rejected once a certain time has passed since death.

Although, strictly speaking, the wishes of someone leaving their body to science cannot be overridden, in reality, doctors will not proceed if there are strong objections from relatives.

Donor Card

I would like to help someone to live after my death.

Let your relatives know your wishes,
and keep this card with you at all times.

DEATH

Many people wishing to donate their body or organs to science indicate this in their will. However, if you decide to do this, it is advisable also to inform a close relative or friend, preferably in writing. Quite often, some time will elapse between death and the location of the will.

Anyone wishing to donate parts of their body for transplant can register with the *Organ Donor Register* - forms are obtainable from post offices, health centres and hospitals. Driving licences issued after October 1994 have provision for holders to indicate whether, in the event of their death, they wish their organs to be used for transplant or to leave their body for medical research. Also available is the Humane Research Donor Card, organised by Animal Aid, allowing the holder to indicate they wish to donate their body for medical research. See **Contacts** for further details of all these schemes.

REGISTERING THE DEATH

There is a duty to register a death within a period of five days. It should be done, in person, by someone who is a *qualified informant*. This is usually the nearest relative or, if there are no relatives, someone else who was present at the death, who was in charge of the place where the death occurred or who is organising the funeral. Registration takes place at the office of the Registrar of Births, Marriages and Deaths. The person registering the death will need to provide full personal details of the deceased, such as date and place of birth, occupation and maiden name. The medical certificate of death and the medical card of the person who died will also be required. If the latter is not available, it can be sent later.

These details can now be provided at *any* registration office and will be forwarded to the Registrar of the district where the death occurred. When a death is registered, a death certificate is issued along with permission for burial or cremation. A further certificate - for social security purposes - is given to the widow, asking whether she would like to claim widow's benefits.

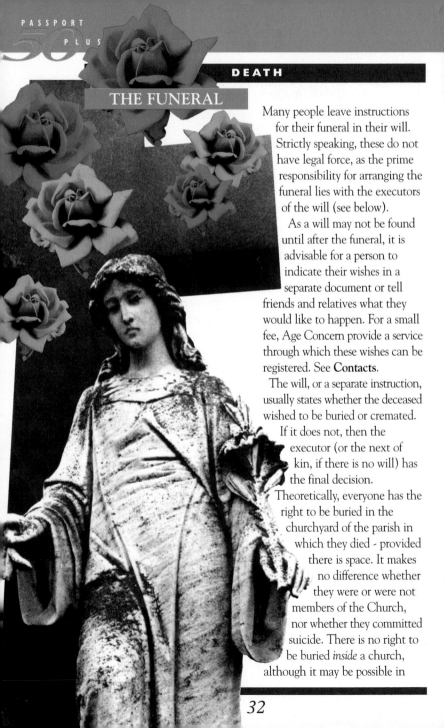

DEATH

THE FUNERAL

Many people leave instructions for their funeral in their will. Strictly speaking, these do not have legal force, as the prime responsibility for arranging the funeral lies with the executors of the will (see below).

As a will may not be found until after the funeral, it is advisable for a person to indicate their wishes in a separate document or tell friends and relatives what they would like to happen. For a small fee, Age Concern provide a service through which these wishes can be registered. See **Contacts**.

The will, or a separate instruction, usually states whether the deceased wished to be buried or cremated. If it does not, then the executor (or the next of kin, if there is no will) has the final decision. Theoretically, everyone has the right to be buried in the churchyard of the parish in which they died - provided there is space. It makes no difference whether they were or were not members of the Church, nor whether they committed suicide. There is no right to be buried *inside* a church, although it may be possible in some rural areas where the church was built before 1848.

Normally, burials take place in Church of England churchyards, cemeteries run by the local authority or in private burial grounds - which are sometimes used by other religious groups. Local authorities may also set aside part of a cemetery for individual denominations. Burial can also take place on private land or a woodland site. Further information can be obtained from the *Institute of Burial and Cremation Administration* and *The Woodland Trust*. See **Contacts** for details.

Someone wishing to be buried on private land (and this could include their own garden), should check local by-laws, the deeds of the property and consult the owner of the land. It is also advisable to contact the Environment Agency (see local 'phone book for details) and the local planning department, who can provide, under the *Town and Country Planning Act 1990*, a *Certificate of Lawfulness*, confirming that the burial is lawful.

Generally, ashes can be scattered anywhere, as long as no offence is committed. Unless they are to be scattered on land where the public has a right of access, the owner of the land should be consulted.

Paying for a funeral

Usually the cost of a funeral is taken from the estate (money and possessions) of the person who has died. Some people take out an insurance policy or belong to a pension scheme which pays a lump sum to cover funeral costs. Others pay for their funeral in advance through a pre-paid funeral plan. It is important to ensure that the executor of the will is aware of the arrangements that have been made.

If you have trouble paying for a funeral that you have to arrange, you may qualify for a *Funeral Payment* to help with the cost. This covers all necessary burial or cremation costs and up to £600 for other funeral expenses. However, it must be paid back from the estate of the person who died.

To qualify, you or your partner must be receiving one of the following benefits: Income Support, income-based Jobseeker's Allowance, Family Credit, Disability Working Allowance, Housing Benefit, Council Tax Benefit and it must

DEATH

be reasonable for you to take responsibility for the funeral expenses. This will usually mean you are the partner of the person who died or a close relative or friend (if they had no partner). The person who died must have been resident in the United Kingdom at the time of their death. Claim forms are available from local Benefit Agency offices.

Before authorising a Payment, the social security office will ask about the financial circumstances of close relatives of the person who has died. A Funeral Payment can be claimed from the date of death and up to three months after the date of the funeral. Payment is by

girocheque made out in the funeral director's name.

If the deceased was a war pensioner help may be available with funeral expenses if death was due to service or the pensioner was receiving:
• a war disablement pension and died in a NHS hospital;
• Constant Attendance Allowance;
• a war pension Unemploy-ability Supplement and an 80% (or more) disablement pension. Claims must be made to the War Pensions Agency within three months of the date of the funeral.

Arrangements for the funeral of someone who dies without relatives or friends will be made by the hospital in which she or he died or by the local council. The hospital or council will also cover the cost of the funeral if no relatives are traced or if relatives are unable to afford the cost themselves and do not qualify for Funeral Payments.

THE WILL

The main purpose of a will is to enable a person to indicate how they would like their money, possessions and property distributed on their death.

DEATH

Making a will

Although it is quite possible to draw up your own will, it is generally advisable to seek help from a solicitor. Mistakes and vagueness over witnessing and wording a will can mean that it is invalid or that problems arise over particular bequests.

The cost of making a will depends on its complexity. If it is relatively straightforward the cost is likely to be £100 - £300. A solicitor will be able to give an estimate of the cost beforehand.

Free legal advice and assistance from a solicitor is available to people whose income and capital are below certain limits and who are aged 70 and over or suffer from particular physical disabilities or a mental disorder. Further details are available from the Citizens Advice Bureau and the Law Society. See **Contacts** for details.

It is important to be clear who will be the main beneficiaries of a will and who will act as executors (usually a close relative or friend, who must be aged 18 or over). Solicitors and banks can be appointed as executors and will usually charge a percentage of the estate as their fee. It is important to check that the person you ask is both willing to and capable of

taking on the responsibilities involved.

A will must be in writing and signed and witnessed by two people. Neither of these people (nor their spouses) must benefit under its terms. It

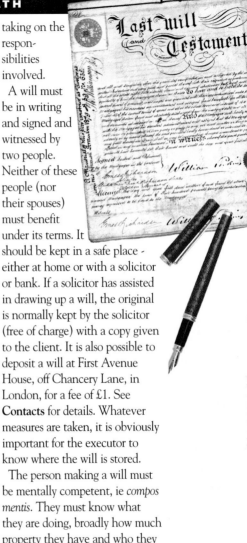

should be kept in a safe place - either at home or with a solicitor or bank. If a solicitor has assisted in drawing up a will, the original is normally kept by the solicitor (free of charge) with a copy given to the client. It is also possible to deposit a will at First Avenue House, off Chancery Lane, in London, for a fee of £1. See **Contacts** for details. Whatever measures are taken, it is obviously important for the executor to know where the will is stored.

The person making a will must be mentally competent, ie *compos mentis*. They must know what they are doing, broadly how much property they have and who they ought to bear in mind in deciding where it all should go. If there is doubt over this, a solicitor should be consulted.

CITIZENSHIP
FOUNDATION

DEATH

Changing a will

A will *automatically* becomes invalid when a person marries or remarries, unless the will was clearly made in the light of a marriage that was soon to take place.

A will is also changed through divorce when bequests to a former husband or wife become invalid. However, under the *Inheritance (Provision for Family and Dependents) Act 1975*, it is possible - although not easy - for some-one who is divorced and has not remarried to challenge the will of their former partner. A will is not altered when couples separate without divorce.

Minor changes to a will may be made through a *codicil* - which is a kind of supplement, adding to or altering the existing will. To be valid, this should, like the original will, be drafted and witnessed in the correct way. A will should never be changed simply by writing alterations on the original document.

The words they use

Administrator	The person dealing with the estate of someone who died without making a will.
Beneficiary	Someone who benefits from a will.
Codicil	A document adding to, varying, or in some way changing part of a will.
Estate	All the money, property and possessions a person owns.
Executor	The person named in a will to deal with a person's affairs.
Grant of probate	A certificate issued by the High Court confirming a person's authority to deal with the assets of someone who has died.
Intestate	The situation when someone dies *without* making a will.
Letters of administration	A formal document giving a person authority to deal with the assets of someone who had died without making a will.
Personal representatives	Executors or administrators.

DEATH

Obtaining probate

After someone dies, the personal representative - that is the *executor* or *administrator* - needs to obtain official permission to distribute the estate. This is known as *the grant of probate*, if the deceased has left a will, and *letters of administration* if he or she has not. The general procedure is the same for both.

• Contact the local probate registry (you should be able to get the address from the public library or the Principal Registry - see **Contacts**), who will send the relevant application forms.

• To complete these, you will need to know personal details of the deceased and the value of their property, finances and other assets. You will also need to indicate whether the deceased had any debts or was owed money by others. This information is used to calculate whether inheritance tax is due on the estate.

• Send the completed forms, with the death certificate and the original will, to the office of the probate registry where you wish to be interviewed. It is advisable to send this by recorded post and to keep copies of everything you send.

• You will be asked to attend at least one informal interview where you will be required to confirm details on the forms you have completed and to swear that the information you have given is correct.

• Following payment of a fee, based on the size of the estate, probate or letters of administration will be granted.

As an executor or administrator, it is advisable to take out a separate bank account into which money from the estate can be placed. It is important to keep an accurate record of what has happened to all the property in the estate.

There is no legal compulsion to act as an executor or administrator - even if, at one stage, you said you would - although it may be difficult to pull out once you have applied for the grant of probate. If the estate is of any size, if it involves a business or partnership, or if it appears that parts of the will may be contested, it is advisable to seek help from a solicitor.

If the value of the estate comes to less than £5,000, or property and assets are in joint names, it may be possible for the estate to be released without the need to apply for probate or letters of administration.

For further information, see form PA 2, *How to obtain probate*, available from a probate registry office.

DEATH

Dying without making a will

Someone who dies without making a will is described as dying intestate. Their property is divided according to a set of general rules. This is a complex area and is a subject upon which many court cases have been contested. However, in very simple terms, the position is as follows.

If the person dies without making a will and....

• was married with no children, the surviving husband or wife is entitled to the first £200,000 of their estate as well as all their personal possessions. Anything else is divided between the surviving spouse (who gets half) and the deceased's parents. If the parents have died, the parents' share passes to the nearest relatives;

• was married with children, then the surviving husband or wife will receive the first £125,000 of the estate and all the personal possessions. The value of the remainder of the estate is shared between the couple's children or grandchildren and the spouse, who gets what is known as a life interest in this share;

• was not married but had a partner. The surviving partner will not normally be entitled to any part of the estate, although the partner can apply to court for a share;

• had no relatives - then the Crown has the right to the whole estate.

Husbands or wives only have a right to inherit under these rules if they survive their partner by at least 28 days. If they do not, their estate consists only of the property they owned before their partner's death.

Forfeiture

Anyone found guilty of causing another person's death is prevented from benefiting under their will. However, this rule has been waived by courts in cases of manslaughter when the person responsible for the death has acted under extreme provocation or bore no responsibility for their actions.

HOME

GRANTS FOR IMPROVEMENTS & REPAIRS

TENANCIES

HARASSMENT & ILLEGAL EVICTION

NOISY NEIGHBOURS

COMMUNITY CARE

SHELTERED HOUSING

RESIDENTIAL & NURSING HOMES

STAYING IN YOUR HOME

As they get older, most people continue to live in their own homes, and it has been the policy of recent governments to encourage this.

GRANTS FOR IMPROVEMENTS AND REPAIRS

Several different types of grants are available for improvements and repairs. Most are means-tested.

In many area there are home improvement agencies able to help people, who are aged 60 or over or who are disabled, with the whole process of arranging and supervising repairs or adaptations to their home. Funded by central and local government, they are sometimes known as Care and Repair or Staying Put - and may be listed under "C" or "S" in the 'phone book.

Renovation grant

This is available to owner-occupiers and tenants whose home either needs structural repairs or lacks facilities such as an inside toilet or a hand basin with hot and cold water. Funds are also available for major repairs to such things as faulty wiring, rotten windows or leaking roofs and other improvements, such as the replacement of a very steep staircase. Grants

may also be obtained for home insulation and the provision of adequate heating. Applicants must have lived in the property for at least three years before they become eligible, and grants are not available for houses built in the last ten years.

If you wish to apply for a grant, contact the renovation grants section at your local council. The success of your application will depend on the council's priorities and on your income and savings. Even if you are above the means-tested limit, you may still qualify for a grant to cover *part* of the cost. If you obtain a grant and then move house within five years, you may have to pay back some or all of the grant.

Home repair assistance

This is designed to help older or disabled home owners, or tenants of private landlords or housing associations who are on a low income to pay for small, but essential, repairs or alterations. It is also the only grant available to people living in mobile homes or on houseboats.

The typical kind of work that might qualify for assistance includes repairs to windows and doors, home security (such as better locks or an intercom system), home insulation, and the installation of a downstairs toilet to allow an older person to move into a friend's or relative's home.

This grant is not usually dependent on a person's income or savings. It is, however, discretionary and councils often have their own checklist of requirements which they use when assessing applications.

Disabled facilities grant

This grant is designed to help a disabled person live as independently as possible. It is available to someone with:
• a substantial sight, hearing or speech impairment;
• a mental disorder or impairment; or
• a substantial physical disability.

Typical of the alterations that might be available under the grant are improved access to the home or to individual rooms, improvements to home safety, heating and lighting, and the provision of suitable bathroom and kitchen equipment for independent living.

Applications for a disabled facilities grant are normally made through either the local housing or social services departments. The grants are means-

> ## Other grants
>
> Grants towards the cost of loft and cavity wall insulation, improved heating controls and energy efficient lamps are available to people aged 60 or over through the *Home Energy Efficiency Scheme*. For more information, contact the Energy Action Grants Agency, see **Contacts** for details.
>
> The *Social Fund* provides grants and loans for minor repairs and redecoration for people on Income Support and income-based Jobseeker's Allowance. Further information is available from your local Benefits Agency office.

tested, but are also mandatory - that is, they **must** be given to someone who is disabled and whose income and savings do not exceed the set level.

Further help is available under the *Chronically Sick and Disabled Persons Act 1970*, which requires local councils to help disabled people through the provision of practical help within the home, disability aids and equipment, and assistance with adaptations to the home. See **Contacts** for details of organisations able to provide further information and advice.

COUNCIL AND HOUSING ASSOCIATION TENANTS

Security of tenure

The right to remain in your own home is called *security of tenure* - and the level of security that a tenant has largely depends on the nature of their tenancy agreement.

If you are a council tenant, or a housing association tenant who moved into your home before 15 January 1989, you will almost certainly have a *secure* tenancy. If you live in housing association property and moved into your home after 15 January 1989, you will probably have an *assured* tenancy. (A few housing association tenants may have an *assured shorthold* tenancy, see page 46). If you are not sure about your tenancy agreement, ask the Citizens Advice Bureau, a housing advice centre or a solicitor to help you sort this out.

Anyone with a *secure* or an *assured* tenancy cannot be made to leave their home unless their landlord obtains a possession order from a court.

Susan was a council tenant and her 13 year old son repeatedly racially harassed a neighbour. The council obtained a possession order on the grounds that this was against Susan's tenancy regulations. Susan appealed against this, arguing that it was not her offensive behaviour that was the problem, but her son's. The Court turned down her appeal. The judge said that justice required that the neighbour's rights should be considered and that the neighbour should not suffer because Susan could not control her son.

If a landlord requires a tenant to leave, he or she must give notice in the correct way. The notice must explain why the tenant is being asked to go and usually must give the tenant a certain amount of time before the landlord applies to the court for a possession order.

The circumstances in which a court may grant a possession order against a tenant include the following:

• the tenant has failed to pay, or been persistently late in paying, rent;

• the tenant has broken the terms of the tenancy agreement, damaged or neglected the property or caused a nuisance to other tenants or other people in the area;

The Council Tenant's Charter

The Council Tenant's Charter explains more about the responsibilities of council's and their tenants. It can be ordered free and is available in large text, audio tape and in a number of different languages. See **Contacts** for details.

STAYING IN YOUR HOME

• the landlord needs to demolish the property or to carry out major repairs which cannot be done while the tenant is still there;

• the home has been designed or adapted for someone with a physical disability, but no one with a disability is living there; or

• the previous tenant has died and the home is larger than the person who has taken over the tenancy needs. This reason can only be used between six and twelve months after the death of the tenant. It can never be used when the person succeeding to the tenancy was a joint tenant or the husband or wife of the tenant.

When a landlord asks a tenant to leave, it is important for the tenant to seek advice as soon as possible. He or she may be quite entitled to stay in their home and a court may well decide that it would be unreasonable to order an eviction.

Council and most housing association tenants have the right to pass their home to another person when they die. Generally, this right extends to their husband or wife or un-married partner, whom they must have lived with for at least a year. It is not open to a partner of the same sex. Tenancies can only be passed on once in this way.

Rent

Local councils have the legal right to fix their own rents. Rent increases must be reasonable.

Housing association tenants who moved into their home before 15 January 1989 should be charged what is called *a fair rent* - as set by the local rent officer. The rent may be raised only if the landlord obtains the tenant's written agreement to increase the rent, or successfully applies to the rent officer for an increase in the rent. Once a fair rent is set, it is fixed for two years.

Housing association tenants who moved into their homes after 15 January 1989 have less protection against rent rises. Most housing association tenants who are assured tenants will have what is known as a *periodic tenancy*, which means that rent is payable at fixed intervals, usually weekly, monthly or quarterly. During the first twelve months of a periodic tenancy, the landlord may increase the rent only if it is allowed for in the tenancy agreement or with the agreement of the tenant. However, after this, the rent may be raised - as long as the tenant is given at least a month's notice of the increase.

If you feel a rent increase is unfair, you can apply to a *rent assessment committee*, which will decide what is a reasonable figure to pay for the rent of your property. There is no charge for this, but it's important to note that the committee can put the rent up as well as down! Once it has been set, the rent cannot be raised again for another year.

Repairs

Responsibility for repairs to the property are set out in the tenancy agreement. Under the *Landlord and Tenant Act 1985*, the landlord is responsible for all repairs to the structure, exterior and essential services (eg. water, electricity, gas) to the property. The only exceptions to this are those tenancies created for a period of more than seven years. The tenant is normally responsible for interior decoration, minor repairs and for damage that he or she has caused.

The council or housing association will have a policy stating the maximum amount of time that tenants should normally have to wait for certain repairs to be done. Further information on this is contained in the *Council Tenant's Charter* and other information leaflets published by the Department of the Environment, Transport and the Regions, see **Contacts** for details.

If the service you receive is not satisfactory and you are unable to settle matters informally, you can report the problem to the council or housing association and follow their complaints procedure, or write to your local councillor. If matters are still not resolved, contact the Local Government Ombudsman or Independent Housing Ombudsman, see **Contacts** for details.

If the disrepair is likely to damage the tenant's health, housing association tenants may report the problem to the local environmental health officer, who has powers to compel a landlord to carry out the repairs. (This action is not open to

council tenants as the council cannot take legal action against itself.)

Legal action by a tenant against a council or housing association should not be seen as a last resort and should not be started before taking legal advice.

Buying or exchanging homes

Most people who have been council tenants for two years have the right to buy their home - although this does not apply to sheltered housing. The discount will be based on the market price of the property and the length of time the tenant has lived in the home, or another council or housing association home.

Both housing association and council tenants have the right to exchange homes with other housing association and council tenants, although there are certain circumstances when this can be refused, for example, if the new home is thought to be too large for the person who wants it. An organisation called HOMES helps to arrange exchanges between tenants who want to move to another part of the country. See **Contacts** for details.

Home letting

Both council and housing association tenants are generally able to take in a lodger or sub-let part of the property, although it is wise for anyone thinking about this to check with their landlord, who must not withhold permission unreasonably. It's also a good idea to inform your insurance company in order to avoid difficulties with any future claims.

PRIVATE TENANTS

The security of tenure for private tenants - that is, their right to stay in their home - depends on the type of agreement they have and whether they are *tenants* or *licensees*.

Tenants are people who have *exclusive possession* of their property or living area, that is, they do not share their home with anyone else other than the

people they choose to live with.

Someone occupying a separate rented flat is clearly a tenant, but so too be can a person living in a bedsitting room, even though they may share the kitchen and bathroom. A **licensee**, on the other hand, is someone who does not have exclusive possession. People living in certain types of accommodation for older people, such as Abbeyfield homes will probably be licensees. If you are not sure whether you are a licensee or tenant, the Citizens Advice Bureau, a housing advice agency, a law centre or a solicitor will be able to help you.

Licensees have less security of tenure than tenants. They can be asked to leave at any time, although the landlord must give them at least four weeks' written notice. In some cases, a landlord requires a possession order to evict a licensee.

Security of tenure

A private tenant's security of tenure largely depends on their type of tenancy. Most tenancies fall into one of three categories: *regulated, assured* or *assured shorthold* tenancies. Most tenancies which started before 15 January 1989 are regulated tenancies. Regulated tenants normally have long term security of tenure and cannot be made to leave their homes unless the landlord can satisfy the court that he or she should be awarded possession of the property under one of the grounds in the *Rent Act 1977*.

Most tenants cannot be made to leave their home unless the landlord obtains a possession order from a court and serves notice to the tenant in the correct way. Generally speaking, grounds for obtaining a possession order include the following:

• the landlord wishes to live in the property as his or her main home (and gave notice of this intention before granting the tenancy);

• the tenant has failed to pay the rent, or has been consistently late in doing so;

• the tenant has broken a condition of the tenancy agreement;

• the tenant has damaged or neglected the property; or

• the tenant is causing a nuisance to neighbours.

It is important to emphasise that a court often has some discretion in deciding whether to grant a possession order. It is not always automatic. In some cases an order will only be granted if the court feels it is reasonable to do so. A tenant may well be entitled to stay in his or her home and the court may decide that it would unreasonable to order an eviction. If a landlord asks a tenant to leave, it is important for the tenant to seek advice as soon as possible.

Harassment and illegal eviction

It is, in most cases, illegal for a landlord to evict a tenant without a court order or to try to force the tenant to leave by making threats. A landlord who behaves in a way designed to force the tenant to leave - like changing the locks or playing loud music - is still committing an offence under the *Protection from Eviction Act 1977*.

Anyone harassed or threatened with eviction should seek advice from a solicitor, the local council or Citizens Advice Bureau, and if physical violence is used or seriously threatened, they should call the police.

STAYING IN YOUR HOME

Rent

Someone with a *regulated* tenancy has the right to apply for what is called a *fair rent*, which is set by a rent officer. Once a fair rent is registered, it cannot be revised for two years unless the landlord or tenant apply jointly or there has been a change of circumstances (eg major repairs). The landlord of someone who is an *assured* or an *assured shorthold* tenant can charge a market rent. If the tenancy is set for a fixed length of time, the landlord cannot raise the rent within this period unless the tenancy agreement allows for this or the tenant agrees. The landlord of a tenant with an *assured* or an *assured shorthold* tenancy of no fixed length (called a periodic tenancy) can raise the rent if it is allowed for in the tenancy agreement or with the consent of the tenant.

Otherwise, he or she must serve a notice on a tenant proposing a new rent. If the tenant thinks the proposed rent is unreasonable, he or she can refer it to the rent assessment committee for them to decide what the rent should be. Once   the committee has set the rent the landlord cannot propose a further rent rise for one year.

Assured shorthold tenants can also apply to the committee during the first six months of their tenancy if they think their rent is significantly higher than the rents for similar tenancies in the area.

Generally, the rent for the licensee arrangements is agreed between the two parties.

Repairs

The need for a repair should be reported to the landlord (preferably in writing) as soon as it becomes apparent. At the same time, it's a good idea for the tenant to be clear about what the tenancy agreement says about their own and the landlord's responsibility for such repairs.

Unless the tenancy agreement is for seven years or more, the landlord is responsible, by law, for looking after the structure and exterior of the building and for certain essential services. Responsibility for other repairs will depend on what is in the tenancy agreement. If, after a reasonable period of time, the landlord fails to carry out repairs, there are a number of courses of action open to the tenant.

If the problem is a risk to health and safety, you can get in touch with the local environmental health office. They have powers to get something done and can make the landlord undertake the necessary work.

If the problem is not sufficiently serious for the local council to take action, check again that responsibility lies with the landlord, and write to the landlord explaining that you intend to undertake the work yourself. At this stage, it is important to keep paying the rent in the usual way. Send the landlord at least two estimates of the cost of the work, giving him or her at least two weeks to query them. If the work has still not been done at the end of this period, you may go ahead with the repairs and deduct the cost from the rent. Keep detailed records of everything that is done and copies of all correspondence.

8 Rose Avenue,
Retford,
Notts. DN22 7HR.

Dear Landlord,

As I told you by (phone/letter) on (date), the water heater at (the address) is broken, and it is your responsibility to put this right under our tenancy agreement. Since this has not been done, I have got (two) estimates for repairs from (names and addresses of firms), which I enclose. Unless I hear from you by (date) that you will do these repairs straightaway, I will have no further option but to ask (name the cheapest firm) to do the repair. I shall then deduct their bill from future rental repayments.

Yours sincerely,

The Tenant

NOISY NEIGHBOURS

The best way to tackle this problem is to approach the person concerned and try to work out a solution. Sometimes this is easier, and more effective, if several people try to raise the complaint together.

If this doesn't work, write to your neighbour (keeping a copy of the letter) explaining the difficulty and give him or her time to respond. If that fails, get in touch with the local environmental health office, which has powers to investigate and deal with such matters under the *Environmental Protection Act 1990*. It is helpful if you can provide a record of the times and ways in which you have been disturbed.

The *Noise Act 1996* gives local authorities special powers to deal with a noise occurring between 11pm and 7am. Local authorities

STAYING IN YOUR HOME

which have chosen to adopt these measures can send an officer to measure the noise and decide whether it is excessive. If it is, the person responsible may be given a warning notice, requiring the noise to be switched off or turned down within 10 minutes. An offence is committed if the noise continues and the officer can decide to prosecute or issue an on-the-spot fine of £100. If the warning notice is ignored, the officer can obtain a warrant to go into the building and remove the sound equipment that is being used.

If the police are called to such a situation, they can ask people to be quiet, but there's not much they can do unless they believe a criminal offence is committed - such as a breach of the peace.

Sometimes the noise may be of a kind that is particularly offensive, with perhaps older people or members of an ethnic minority as its target. Most tenancy agreements have clauses preventing tenants from creating a nuisance and, under the *Housing Act 1996*, councils and housing associations can now evict tenants causing an annoyance to people living in or visiting the area. See page 42.

COMMUNITY CARE SERVICES

What is community care?

Community care is designed to provide the services and support to help a person live independently at home or in "homely" surroundings wherever this can be done. The services may be provided by different groups, including social services departments, the Health Service, voluntary and private organisations. The process may be started by a doctor, district nurse, a family member, a carer, or the person concerned who contacts the local social services department to say that help may be required.

How is it arranged?

Local authority social service departments have overall responsibility for planning and arranging community care services. They are responsible for assessing a person's needs and then arranging the necessary care.

Local authorities are under a

legal duty under the *National Health and Community Care Act 1990* to give a community care assessment to anyone who, in the authority's view, may be in need of community care services. A disabled person, however, must be given an assessment by the local authority if he or she requests it. Anyone who thinks they should have been given an assessment, but were refused one, can use the local authority's complaints procedure.

The way in which the assessment is carried (including the number and type of staff involved) will vary from person to person, and the authority will decide what is appropriate in each case. Sometimes a very quick and simple assessment will provide all the information necessary. The person concerned should be consulted about what *they* feel their needs are, and about the kind of help they would like to receive. Government guidance emphasises that care services should be devised and provided in a way that meets the person's need - and not be primarily determined by what is most convenient for the local authority.

After the assessment, the person concerned should be

given a written record of the assessment and care plan, including details of how and when the services will be provided.

Carers who provide, or intend to provide, a substantial amount of care on a regular basis are also entitled to request an assessment of their ability to care, at the same time. The results of this are then taken into account when decisions are made about the type and level of services to be provided for the person receiving care.

Paying for care

It is for each local authority to decide what charges to make for non-residential services. Some services are provided free, but others are means-tested and charges imposed vary from one area to another.

MOVING HOME

But there is usually an upper limit to what is paid and rates must be "reasonable". Unless it is an emergency, a person should be told about the charges for their care when they are offered the service. Someone who feels they are being charged too much or who finds difficulty in paying should raise the matter straightaway.

Complaints

If you are critical of the way an assessment was carried out, the decision that was reached or the way in which your care is being provided, it's important to raise the matter as soon as possible. It's usually better to start at the local level, but if the problem is not resolved you can use either the social services department's complaints procedure or the NHS Complaints Procedure, if your complaint involves the health service. Further information on this is available from your local Community Health Council and the *Community Care Charter*.

MOVING HOME

The main options open to someone wishing to move during the later stages of their life are listed below.

SMALLER HOUSING

A flat or smaller house is a possibility for someone whose home has become too large for their needs. The property can be rented or purchased in the normal way. There is no age limit to taking on a mortgage as long as the bank or building society is satisfied that the monthly payments can be managed. Interest only mortgages are also available, designed for older people who need to  raise a little extra capital to buy a new home. Interest is only paid on the loan. The capital need not be repaid until the house is eventually sold.

MOVING HOME

SHELTERED HOUSING

Sheltered housing is provided by councils, housing associations and private developers, and may be available to rent or buy. Wardens are sometimes resident but do not provide help with washing, cleaning, cooking or personal care - although separate community care services can be arranged. A small number of schemes are specifically run for elderly people from Afro-Caribbean or Asian communities. Some other schemes also offer independent living, but with the provision of prepared food each day.

The facilities in private sheltered housing schemes are usually run by a separate management organisation. It is important, therefore, to be aware of the terms and financial implications of these arrangements before going ahead with the purchase or lease.

For example, if the scheme has been running for some years, you can ask to see a record of previous charges. The Advice, Information and Mediation Service offers advice for owner-occupiers and leaseholders of sheltered housing, see **Contacts** for details.

RESIDENTIAL AND NURSING HOMES

These are run by councils, charities, housing associations and private owners, providing food, accommodation and personal care and, with nursing homes, 24-hour medical care. Most residential and nursing homes are required to be registered by law and have to be inspected at least twice a year. Copies of the inspection reports are available for the public to read and are obtainable from the local authority's Inspection and Registration Unit. Local social services departments will hold copies of reports on residential homes in the area, and reports on nursing homes will be held by the Health Authority.

CITIZENSHIP
FOUNDATION

MOVING HOME

Choosing a home

The social services department, library or Citizens Advice Bureau are able to provide a list of local residential and nursing homes. A register of nursing homes will also be held by the local Health Authority. Age Concern and other charities concerned with older people can also help.

Age Concern and social services departments stress the importance of looking

MOVING IN WITH RELATIVES

There are clearly a number of factors to consider before doing this, particularly if property is to be sold or a lease relinquished. If the arrangement doesn't work, it will be impossible to put things back as they were. If either side puts capital into the new arrangement, it is advisable for both parties to take separate legal advice, and to draw up some kind of clear enforceable agreement.

It is not uncommon for an older person, thinking that they might live with their daughter or son, to contemplate either making a gift of their home or selling it, in order to fund the purchase of a new property. A gift may have advantages, as far as inheritance tax is concerned, but gives little security to the elderly parent. It is very important for both sides to take legal advice on this in order to be aware of the various financial and legal implications. It is also preferable for this to be given by *different* solicitors, in order to ensure that, should the living arrangements break down, the solicitor does not face the problem of giving advice to one of his or her clients which conflicts with the interests of another.

MOVING HOME

around and comparing more than one home. While you or your family may prefer to make an appointment with the home before visiting, there is no problem in arriving unannounced (assuming that it is not at an unreasonable hour), as a means of seeing the home working in a normal way. When you do look round, it's useful to have a list of questions you would like answered. These might, for example, concern residents' independence, privacy, choice and control, their diet, personal possessions, medical care and facilities. It's also obviously important to reflect on the "feel" of the home and how residents are treated by various members of staff. A checklist of useful questions is available from Age Concern and many local authorities.

If a local authority is making the arrange- ments for someone to move into a home, it remains important that the person's views and wishes are taken into account. Ideally they should be told about all the homes in the area that are suitable for their needs. If they do not like the home suggested, they are quite entitled to ask the authority to arrange for a place in the home of their choice - which is called their *preferred accommodation*. The authority must follow this request, as long as the home is suitable for the person's needs, a place is available, the place does not cost more than the authority would normally pay for someone with such needs, and the home is willing to enter into a contract with the authority.

55

FINANCIAL ARRANGEMENTS

Most older people moving into a residential or nursing home make a contribution towards the cost of their care. If they have more than £16,000 capital, or a high enough income, they will be expected to pay the full cost of their care. This will continue until that person's savings fall to £16,000 or their income is reduced. A small number of older people, however, need the kind of care that meets their Health Authority's criteria for continuing in-patient care. Under these circumstances, all the hospital or nursing home costs will be met by the National Health Service.

The level of contribution that a person, whose costs are not being met by the NHS, will be expected to make is calculated using standard rules, which take into account their income and capital. Leaflets explaining this are available from local social services departments, the Health Authority, the Citizens Advice Bureau and most libraries. Generally the amount paid will cover everything you would expect a care home to provide, but it is worth checking exactly what the weekly fee includes, whether there are any hidden extras and what happens if, for example, the resident has to go into hospital or goes away on holiday. If you have any doubts over a contract you are being asked to sign, seek legal advice.

If you own your own home, its value will generally be included when your capital is calculated, unless the following people are still living there:
• your husband, wife or partner;
• a relative who is 60 or over, or incapacitated; or
• a relative who is under 16, whom you are legally obliged to support.

It is up to you whether you sell your home. However, until your property is sold, the social services department may place a charge on your property, whereby they contribute towards your fees and recover what they have paid after the sale. They cannot make you sell your property, unless they obtain a court order.

If your capital falls to £16,000 and your income is not sufficient to meet the fees in full, you should apply to the local authority social services department. The local authority will assess your care needs and can then, if the home is suitable, make a contract with the home for your care. If the cost of the care in the home is higher than the authority normally pays, they will probably suggest a place for you in another home, unless there someone else who is able to cover the difference - perhaps a relative or a charity.

WORK
& RETIREMENT

EQUAL RIGHTS

CONTRACTS

PART-TIME WORK

HEALTH & SAFETY

LOSING YOUR JOB

VOLUNTARY WORK & EDUCATION

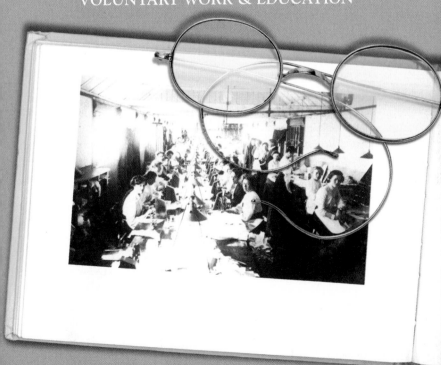

EQUAL RIGHTS

In most situations at work, it is unlawful for an employer to treat someone unfairly because of their gender, race, skin colour, nationality or disability. The law applies to people in both full and part-time work. Discrimination on the basis of age is not illegal.

Often discrimination at work is obvious. A person who is not treated as well as someone else because of their skin colour, gender etc. suffers what is called **direct discrimination**. But sometimes the situation is more subtle, such as when the conditions or terms imposed by an employer unfairly limit the chances of people who fall into a particular category. This is called **indirect discrimination**.

Direct

Eugene suffered constant racist taunts by other workers on the building site where he worked, but the management did little to stop it. They said that "black bastard" and "nigger" were words often used on sites. An industrial tribunal disagreed, saying the company should have taken a much firmer line on this. The tribunal decided that Eugene had been **directly discriminated** against. He was awarded £2000 damages.

Indirect

Belinda wanted to return to work part-time after having a baby. The magazine company where she worked said that this was not possible. Belinda took her case to an industrial tribunal, claiming that, by saying the work had to be done on a full-time basis, the employer was applying a condition with which fewer women than men can comply. The case eventually reached the Employment Appeal Tribunal, which agreed with Belinda and decided that the policy **indirectly discriminated** against women.

SEX DISCRIMINATION

Under the *Sex Discrimination Act 1975* it is unlawful to discriminate against a person on grounds of their sex or being married. The law applies to members of either sex. It covers all aspects of work - including job applications, training, promotion etc., but does allow exceptions to be made when sex is a genuine occupational qualification. It would not be against the law, for example, for the post of an attendant in a female lavatory to be open only to women.

The *Equal Pay Act 1970* states that men and women are entitled to the same pay and conditions when doing the same job or one of equal value. The time limit for complaints about unequal pay is six months.

Until recently, the law has allowed discrimination on grounds of sexual orientation. For example, it has not been unlawful to refuse to employ a man because he was homosexual. However, following a recent case heard by the European Court, it is now likely that discrimination in employment on grounds of sex will include sexual orientation and that this, too, will become unlawful.

A person who feels they are a victim of unfair sexual discrimination at work can make a complaint to an industrial tribunal, but this needs to be done within three months of the incident.

After a long running battle with their employers, Durham City Council, 28 women who worked as wardens in sheltered accommodation succeeded in their claim that their work was of equal value to that of many of their male colleagues. As a result, they gained a 35% increase in wages and shared back pay and compensation worth £400,000.

Equal Opportunities Commission

Information and advice on all forms of sexual discrimination is available from the Equal Opportunities Commission, see **Contacts** for details.

Unwelcome Attention

Many people, at some stage in their working lives, receive unwanted sexual attention from colleagues. Sexual harassment covers a whole range of things, from rude remarks to leering and unwanted physical contact. In law it is seen as **direct discrimination**, under the *Sex Discrimination Act 1975*. Although it happens more often to women, men can be victims too.

It is probably best to try at first to sort things out personally. But if the harassment continues, don't be afraid to complain. It is not always easy to prove in court, but judges are now prepared to award damages when the victim can show that they have suffered some disadvantage or injury to their feelings from the sexual harassment. Complaints can be brought against both an individual and an employer.

RACIAL DISCRIMINATION

Under the *Race Relations Act 1976*, it is unlawful for an employer to discriminate unfairly against either an employee or applicant for a job because of their race, colour, nationality, citizenship or ethnic origin.

However, the law does not apply when the employment is in a private household or when certain racial or ethnic characteristics are needed for a particular job - such as an actor, model or waiter in an ethnic restaurant.

Someone who feels they have been unfairly discriminated against at work should contact their trade union or professional association or the Citizens Advice Bureau. Advice and information is also available from the Commission for Racial Equality. If matters cannot be sorted informally, the complaint may be taken to an industrial tribunal. The application for this must be made within three months of the incident taking place. See **Contacts** for details.

DISABILITY DISCRIMINATION

The *Disability Discrimination Act 1995* is designed to protect disabled people, and people who have had a disability, from unfair discrimination. The main provisions of the Act relating to employment started to come into effect in 1996.

The employment rights apply to firms of 20 or more employees who must not treat a disabled person less favourably than other people, unless that treatment can be justified. The law also states that a firm may have to make reasonable adjustments to their premises or employment arrangements to enable a disabled person to do their job.

Anyone who feels they may have been unlawfully discriminated against because of their disability can obtain help from a number of organisations, such as the Citizens Advice Bureau, their

trade union and the Disability Law Service. Information is also available from the Disability Discrimination Information Line and from ACAS (the Advisory, Conciliation and Arbitration Service) which can also offer to help in settling the dispute. See **Contacts** for details.

If the matter cannot be resolved, individuals have the right to take their complaint to an industrial tribunal - but the application should be made within three months of the original incident.

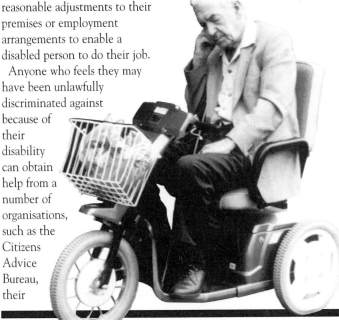

CONTRACTS

Everyone at work has a contract - whether in full- or part-time employment. The contract is an agreement between an employee and employer, spelling out the arrangements for work - such as pay, hours, the kind of job that will be done, holidays and the notice to be given when the employment comes to an end.

Contracts don't have to be in writing. They can be agreed verbally - but it's important to get something on paper, in case there's disagreement over what either side can expect of the other in particular situations.

IN WRITING

Someone who is employed for more than a month, **must**, within two months of starting work, be given a written statement by their employer, setting out the terms and conditions of the job.

This statement should show:
• the job title and place of work;
• the date when the job begins,
• the rate of pay, and how it will be paid;
• hours of work;
• holidays and holiday pay;
• arrangements for sick pay and pension;

• details of the firm's disciplinary procedures, (only if 20 or more people are employed), and how complaints at work are to be dealt with; and
• the amount of notice that must be given if the contract is to be ended.

Take Care

If you regularly agree to do something that is not written into your contract - such as working on a Saturday - you may, in law, be agreeing to this new term or condition of work. If, later you decide that working every Saturday is not a good idea, your boss may be entitled to insist that you continue. By turning up for work six days a week, you may have actually changed your contract by your conduct.

PAY

Employees are entitled to a written pay statement showing exactly what they are being paid and how much is being taken off in tax and insurance etc.. It is up to the employer to choose whether the money will be paid by cash, cheque, or straight into a bank account.

Rates of sick pay must be explained in the contract. Most people who are under 65 and

CONTRACTS

earning above a certain limit will be entitled to Statutory Sick Pay if they are sick for more than four days. The rates are set by Parliament each year and details are published in leaflets available from Social Security offices, libraries and Citizens Advice Bureaux. Many employers have their own sick pay scheme, which will be at least as good as Statutory Sick Pay and may be paid instead of, or in conjunction with it.

Minimum Pay

Until a few years ago there were agreed minimum wages for a number of jobs, including shopwork. These have been abolished, and minimum pay rates now apply to farmwork only. Employers can generally offer whatever wages they wish. However, this is likely to change when plans for a national minimum wage are implemented.

PART-TIME WORK

In 1994, senior judges decided that UK laws unfairly discriminated against part-time workers. As a result, many of the rights of those in part-time jobs (even if it's for only a couple of hours per week) are the same as those of people in full-time employment. If you are in part-time work you:

• are protected by the discrimin-

INDUSTRIAL ACTION

Someone taking industrial action - eg by stopping work - may be breaking their contract of employment. If they are, the employer has the right to dismiss them. But it is important that all strikers are treated in the same way. If one striker is dismissed and others are not, that person may have a case for unfair dismissal.

This protection only applies to strikes that have been lawfully organised and correctly balloted. Unfair dismissal cannot be claimed by someone sacked for taking part in an unofficial strike.

ation laws, regardless of how many hours you work or how long you have worked for your employer;

• have the right, after working for one month, to be given notice if asked to leave, and within two months to be given the terms and conditions of your job in writing;

• are entitled to redundancy pay if you are made redundant and have worked for your employer for at least two years; and

• are entitled to claim for unfair dismissal if you have worked for your employer for at least two years and feel you have been unfairly sacked.

HEALTH & SAFETY

TAKING CARE

Under the *Health and Safety at Work Act 1974*, employers have a legal duty to take care of the health, safety and welfare of their staff.

This means that equipment must not be dangerous or defective, other employees must work safely and responsibly, and there must be adequate supervision and proper instruction. In a firm with five or more employees, the employer must record details of the health and safety arrangements in *writing*.

If you are concerned about health and safety at work, it should be raised with the firm's health and safety representative or a senior member of staff.

If the matter is not resolved, you can contact the local offices of the Health and Safety Executive or the local authority, if you work in a service industry. The Citizens Advice Bureau can explain how to do this.

ACCIDENTS

Anyone injured at work should immediately report the matter to their supervisor and, unless the injury is very small, see a doctor. It's important to make a note of what happened and also to seek legal advice from a trade union, solicitor or the Citizens Advice Bureau, who will also be able to tell you whether you are entitled to any welfare benefits. Any firm with more than ten employees must keep an accident record book.

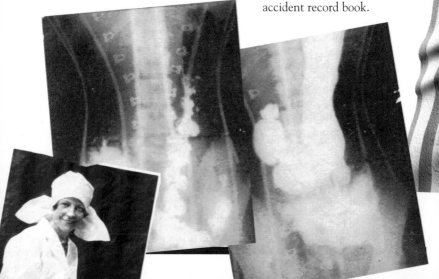

HEALTH & SAFETY

Irene worked as a secretary for many years in an office where several of her colleagues smoked. Though a nonsmoker herself, she felt no ill effects as the area was well ventilated. However, the situation deteriorated when Irene and other people in her section were moved to another part of the building, where the smoke and smell from the cigarettes could not be dispelled. Despite knowing her concern, Irene's employer did nothing to discourage people from smoking or to create a more comfortable working environment. After complaining for almost three years, she eventually left and found another job, but decided to take her case to an industrial tribunal claiming unfair dismissal. Irene argued that she had been forced to leave because of her employer's failure to provide satisfactory working conditions. The tribunal agreed - an employer has a duty to provide a working environment which is suitable for employees to carry out their work in.

Barry worked in a butcher's and was cutting meat when his hand slipped, taking off the top of two fingers. His boss had often told him to use a special guard - but the others at work didn't do it, so Barry didn't bother either. He was awarded damages in court because his employer did not make sure that he was working in the right way, but they were reduced by a third because Barry hadn't followed the safety instructions.

LOSING YOUR JOB

NOTICE

Unless you have done something very serious and committed *gross misconduct* - eg theft - your boss should not sack you on the spot. Your contract should state the notice to which you are entitled, which usually depends on how long you have been working for your employer.

After one month's employment, either side should give one week's notice. After two years' employment, the notice the employer must give goes up to two weeks, to three weeks after three years, and so on, up to twelve weeks' notice for employment lasting twelve years or more. However, an employee's or employer's entitlement to notice may be longer if this is stated in the contract. An employer is generally entitled to pay off a worker, rather than allowing him or her to work out their notice.

REASONS IN WRITING

If you are fired by an employer for whom you have worked for more than two years, you can ask for a written statement of the reasons for your dismissal. This must be provided by your employer within 14 days.

ILL HEALTH

If persistent or prolonged sickness or injury prevents someone from doing their job, there may come a stage when their employer decides to dismiss them. In such circumstances the employee may have a case for unfair dismissal.

In considering this, a tribunal would look at a number of factors, including the procedure the employer followed before dismissal, the nature of the illness, how long it was likely to continue, the nature of the employee's job, length of service and the importance of finding a replacement. Anyone in this position should seek advice from their trade union, the Citizens Advice Bureau or a solicitor as soon as possible.

If you are away from work for any length of time, it's important

We regret to inform you that your services will no longer be needed. Yours sincerely,

to keep your employer fully informed of the medical position and to make it clear that you intend to return to work.

UNFAIR DISMISSAL

If you feel that you have been unfairly dismissed, and have worked for your employer continuously for two years or more, you can make a complaint to an industrial tribunal. It makes no difference whether you are full- or part-time, although claims for unfair dismissal cannot be made beyond the normal retirement age for your employment.

In certain circumstances, no qualifying period of employment is needed to make an unfair dismissal claim - for instance, if the dismissal is on grounds of trade union membership, non-membership or activism.

If you've not been sacked, but leave your job because of the behaviour of your employer, you may also have a claim for unfair dismissal. This is known in law as *constructive dismissal*, but will be successful only if you can show that your employer has broken your employment contract. If you are thinking of resigning because of this, keep a record of what is happening

and, before you hand in your notice, write to your employer explaining your reasons for leaving.

Take legal advice before you make a claim for unfair dismissal, and particularly before resigning. Your trade union, local Citizens Advice Bureau, or a solicitor can help you. If you are unhappy about your dismissal, don't delay seeking assistance. **You only have three months in which to make a complaint.**

If the tribunal agrees that a dismissal is unfair, the employer will probably be ordered to pay the employee money in compensation. This is based on a sliding scale of entitlement (*max £6,300, January 1998*), plus a figure for compensation, based on how long it will take the claimant to find work (*max £11,300, January 1998*). Only in rare cases will a tribunal order an employer to reinstate someone who has been unfairly dismissed.

There are no limits to the damages that may be awarded to someone who has lost their job through through unfair racial, sexual or disability discrimination.

LOSING YOUR JOB

Jeannette's son was ill during the night and, as a consequence, next morning she overslept. When she arrived late at the petrol station where she worked, her boss told her she had been fired. She explained the reason for her lateness, but to no avail. Jeannette took her case to an industrial tribunal, where it was decided that she had been unfairly dismissed. Her lateness did not merit immediate dismissal - she should have been given a warning and another chance.

REDUNDANCY

Redundancy occurs when an employee's services are no longer required. That is, when:
• the business for which the person was employed ceases;
• the business is moved to another place; or
• the need for the kind of work undertaken by the employee declines or is no longer required. Employees who have been laid off or kept on short time without pay for four consecutive weeks (or for six weeks in a period of 13 weeks), are entitled to end their employment and seek redundancy, if there is no reasonable prospect that normal work will be resumed.
The level of payment depends mainly on the employee's age and the length of time they have worked for the business.

You have a right to redundancy pay if you:
• have worked for your employer for a continuous period of at least two years from the age of 18, and
• are under retirement age, and
• have not unreasonably turned down an offer of another job from your employer.
Redundancy payments are not available to employees who have reached 65 or the normal retirement age - whichever comes sooner.

If your employer's company has folded or is in financial difficulty, you may be able to obtain a redundancy payment from the Department of Trade and Industry Redundancy Payment Service.

If you feel that the way you were chosen for redundancy was unfair or unreasonable, you may be able to claim unfair dismissal. The procedure for this is explained on page 67.

Under the *Employment Rights Act 1996*, an employer intending to make 20 or more workers redundant over a period of 90 days or less must consult with

LOSING YOUR JOB

employees' representatives over ways of reducing the number of redundancies. There are also regulations over the procedure to be followed in the event of job losses through the transfer of a business, such as a takeover. Employees who believe that their employer has failed to take the appropriate steps may submit a claim to an industrial tribunal. If they are successful, the employer can be ordered to pay a *protective award*. This requires the employer to pay the employees covered by the award their normal week's pay for each week of the specified period - in addition to any redundancy pay.

Information

If you are made redundant, it is wise to seek advice from a trade union, Citizens Advice Bureau

Redundancy Payments Service Charter, available free from the Department of Trade and Industry Redundancy Payments Service, see **Contacts**.

If you are made redundant, or leave work before the normal retirement age, it is important to consider the likely effect of this on your pension. Information will be available from your company pension scheme manager, pensions consultants and the Occupational Pensions Advisory Service, see **Contacts**. The subject of pensions is dealt with in some detail on pages 74 - 79.

The *Jobseeker's Charter* sets out standards members of the public can expect from the Employment Service when they are looking for a job.

or
a solicitor
as soon as possible.
Rights to a redundancy
payment are explained in the

CITIZENSHIP
FOUNDATION

LOSING YOUR JOB

RETIREMENT

The age at which a person must retire is usually determined by their contract of employment, and must apply equally to men and women. Retirement age is not necessarily the same as state pension age. Some people with occupational pensions are eligible to draw their pension before 65, and women are currently able to obtain their state pension from the age of 60 (although by the year 2020 this too will have been raised to the age of 65). For more information on pensions, see pages 74 - 79.

If you retire before state pension age, and are below the age of 60, you should ensure that you protect your national insurance record by signing on or sending in a sick note.

Once they reach 60,

men are automatically credited with national insurance contributions, provided they are not liable to pay contributions through their employment or self-employment.

Continuing to work

There is normally nothing to  stop anyone working after state pension age - although some occupations and organisations do have upper age limits for their employees.

If you do decide to continue to work, you can choose whether to draw your pension or to defer it until a later date. Your pension will not be affected by the amount you earn or the number of hours you work. However, it will count as part of your taxable income.

Anyone working after reaching state pension age does not need to pay national insurance contributions. You can get a certificate of exemption (CF384), to hand to your employer, from the Department of Social Security.

You can continue working without claiming retirement pension for a period of up to five years, and receive an increased pension as a result. Help on working out whether this is worthwhile is given in *A Guide to Retirement Pensions*, leaflet NP46, issued by the Benefits Agency and available from libraries and Citizens Advice Bureaux.

For employees who pass the age of 65, two significant legal rights are withdrawn. There is no right to protection against unfair dismissal when an employee has exceeded the normal retiring age for that position or, in any other case, the age of 65. Nor do those over 65 have a right to receive redundancy compensation.

People who are self-employed may continue to work as long as they wish, as may members of a partnership. However, the partnership does not automatically fold if old age or mental incapacity prevents a partner from carrying out his or her duties - although these do provide grounds for dissolving the partnership by court decree.

There is no upper age limit for someone acting as a director of a private company - but some companies do stipulate upper age limits for their directors. However, there are restrictions on people aged 70 or over being appointed or continuing as a director of a public company.

ALTERNATIVES TO WORK

VOLUNTARY WORK

A wide range of tasks can be undertaken, benefiting both volunteers and the people for whom they are working. Opportunities for part-time voluntary work exist in many walks of life and most organisations are prepared to look for a mutually convenient arrangement.

Lists of local voluntary organisations and charities are available from libraries and the Citizens Advice Bureau. Most areas also have a volunteer bureau to help people find work.

The Retired and Senior Volunteer Programme (RSVP) encourages people over 50 to participate in volunteering. REACH offers a free job-finding service throughout England and Wales, putting retired business and professional people in touch with charities. See **Contacts** for details of both organisations.

EDUCATION

Many opportunities exist for older people to develop or extend their education, either formally or informally. There is no upper age limit to places on courses at the local adult education centre, further education college or university.

The Open University and the Open College of the Arts (OCA) offer a wide range of courses which can be studied at home, with local tutorial support. Courses run by the OCA can be graded and put towards a university qualification.

Organisations such as the Workers' Education Authority, the Women's Institute and the University of the Third Age all run a national network of centres offering a wide range of courses.

The local library is the best place to start to find out information on courses available in your area, and see **Contacts** for further details.

MONEY

PENSIONS

BENEFITS

BANKS

INSURANCE

TAX

CLAIMING A PENSION

Approximately four months before reaching pensionable age (currently 60 for women and 65 for men)everyone is sent a pension claim form. If they do not receive one, they should contact their local Benefits Agency office. Women's state pension age will be increased gradually from 60 to 65 between the years 2010 and 2020. Women born before 6 April 1950 will not be affected.

There are three separate parts to the Retirement Pension, although not everybody qualifies for each one: a *Basic Pension*, a *Graduated Retirement Benefit*, and an *Additional Pension*.

THE BASIC PENSION

Everyone who has reached pensionable age and has paid, or been credited with, sufficient National Insurance contributions should receive a Basic Pension.

Whether they receive the full Basic Pension depends on their level of contributions and, in particular, whether they have accrued enough *qualifying years* during their working life. A *qualifying year*, for the Basic Pension, is a tax year in which a person has earned at least 52 times the lower earnings limit for that year, and paid National Insurance contributions on these earnings.

For example, if a person is to have 1997-98 as a *qualifying year* they must have earned at least £3,224 (52 x the lower earnings limit of £62 which applied in that year).

To receive a full Basic Pension, about nine out of every ten years of a person's working life need to be *qualifying years*.

Someone unable to pay National Insurance contributions through, for example, unemployment, sickness or disability, may receive credits in place of a contribution - although it is important to note that certain conditions may apply.

GRADUATED RETIREMENT BENEFIT

Graduated Retirement Benefit is based on the amount of graduated NI

Married women

A married woman who has not paid enough contributions to receive a Basic Pension in her own right may be entitled to claim a married woman's pension based on her husband's contribution record. However, this type of pension is only payable to the wife once the husband reaches pensionable age and starts drawing his pension.

contributions paid between 1961 and 1975. If you were employed during any part of this period and paid graduated contributions, you will get a Graduated Retirement Benefit. The amount received depends on the number of units paid and their value at the time the pension is claimed.

ADDITIONAL PENSION

The additional pension is the earnings-related part of the state Retirement Pension, more commonly known as SERPS (*State Earning-Related Pension Scheme*). Introduced in 1978, it provides a top-up to the basic pension and is calculated on the proportion of a person's earnings between the upper and lower National Insurance earnings limits in each tax year.

However, under the *Pensions Act 1995*, the extra benefits available from SERPS are being progressively reduced from 25% to 20% of qualifying earnings. The SERPS scheme is only open to people in employment making full National Insurance contributions.

Since 1988, employees have had the option of contracting out of SERPS and having their contributions paid into an employer's contracted-out private pension scheme instead. It is possible for people who contract out of SERPS to rejoin later.

FORECASTING YOUR PENSION

The Retirement Pensions Forecast and Advice Service enables you to check the level of your state pension contributions and how much you are likely to receive when you retire. Applications can be made up to four months before you reach pensionable age, on form BR 19, *Request for a Retirement Pension Forecast*, available from local Benefits Agency and Social Security offices.

Any gaps in your contributions record may be made up by making a late contribution (this must generally be done before the sixth tax year after the year in which it was due).

Furthermore, if you know that you will be abroad or not paying contributions for a while, it may be worth thinking about making voluntary contributions in order to boost your contributions record.

PAYMENT

You can collect your pension each week in advance from a post office or have it paid in arrears into a bank, Girobank, building society, or investment account with the National Savings Bank. Under the second option you can choose to receive it every four or every 13 weeks. A pension order cannot be cashed more than three months after the date printed on it.

If you cannot get to a post office, your pension book gives details of how someone else can cash your pension for you.

WORKING PAST PENSIONABLE AGE

On reaching pensionable age, you can draw your State Pension. If you carry on working and earning past pensionable age, your State Pension will not be affected. Your pension will be treated as part of your income for tax purposes and you will no longer be required to pay National Insurance contributions.

DELAYING YOUR PENSION

You can defer your pension for up to five years past your pensionable age in order to earn extra pension. The extra earned is currently about 7.5% per full year that you do not draw it. This means that a full five year deferment will increase your pension by about 37.5%. In fact, even if you start drawing your pension you can change your mind and defer it. However, this decision can only be made once.

OCCUPATIONAL PENSIONS

Many employers have occupational pension schemes. Under recent law, these must treat both sexes equally and must be open to both full- and part-time employees. However, some groups may be excluded, such as employees under 25 and high earning executives.

A pension is normally payable when an employee has reached a certain age (usually 60-65) or completed a set length of service. Early retirement is possible under most schemes although, as a result, the pension will usually be reduced. Employers must give information about their pension scheme to all employees eligible to join.

An occupational pension is usually paid monthly and is subject to income tax. Most schemes allow employees to take a tax-free cash lump sum at retirement - although this does reduce the size of the regular pension.

There are two main types of occupational pension - money purchase and final salary schemes. A **money purchase** scheme is based on a fixed rate of contribution, usually a percentage of the employee's salary. Contributions continue for as long as the employee remains a member of the scheme and are invested by the scheme's trustees. The final pension will depend on the amount the employee has paid into the

PENSIONS

scheme (often including a contribution from the employer) and the result of the investment.

Final salary schemes provide pensions which are a proportion of an employees' earnings at or near retirement and are linked to the number of years an employee has been working for the company.

Leaving the company

Contributions to a company pension end when an employee leaves the company. Someone who has been a member of a scheme for less than two years, can claim a cash refund of contributions made, less certain deductions. Employees who have belonged to a scheme for longer than this will be entitled - at pensionable age - to the pension benefits earned before leaving.

Alternatively, an employee may transfer the sum accrued to another occupational pension, run by his or her new employer or to a personal pension scheme (see below).

If you have an occupational pension, it is important to notify the managers of the scheme when you become eligible to draw it. Failure to claim a pension within six years of its maturity can mean that the payments will be reduced.

PERSONAL PENSIONS

Available to both employees and the self-employed, personal pensions are fully portable from job to job and are built up through an individual's regular contributions. They are operated by life insurance companies and other authorised financial institutions which invest the contributions to provide subscribers with an income on retirement and benefits for dependents in the event of the holder's death.

Personal pensions use the **money purchase** scheme and, like occupational pensions, provide the option of taking a tax-free cash lump sum on retirement.

As an employee, it is possible to add to your pension by contracting out of the state earnings-related pension scheme (SERPS) and transferring that proportion of your National Insurance contributions to fund your personal pension. However, before taking action on this it is important to take professional advice from an independent financial adviser.

There is evidence that, since 1988, when they were first introduced, a significant number of personal pensions have been sold or transferred incorrectly. Financial service firms have been instructed by their regulators not to destroy any files relating to personal pension plans sold to people transferring from occupational schemes. Companies selling pensions and offering advice are now more closely regulated than in the past - but, before purchasing a personal pension, it is still vital to seek advice from an authorised pension provider or specialist consultant. A free information service is available from the *Occupational Pensions Advisory Service*, an independent voluntary organisation with local advisors who are experienced in pension matters. See **Contacts** for details.

PENSIONS DISPUTES

If you have a complaint or dispute about an occupational or personal pension, it should be first raised with the manager of the scheme or your employer, as appropriate. If you are not satisfied, you should approach the *Occupational Pensions Advisory Service*.

If the problem is still unresolved, you should write to the *Pensions Ombudsman* who can investigate complaints of injustice over maladministration or disputes of fact or law. If your complaint comes within this brief, the Pensions Ombudsman will initiate an investigation and, if appropriate, will decide on a remedy.

The Pensions Ombudsman should be contacted within three years of the action or failure upon which the complaint is based. See **Contacts** for further details.

CITIZENSHIP
FOUNDATION

BENEFITS

UNEMPLOYED AND ACTIVELY SEEKING WORK

The Jobseeker's Allowance has replaced Unemployment Benefit and Income Support for people who are unemployed and is made up of two elements: one based on National Insurance contributions and the other income-based. To qualify, a person must generally be under pensionable age, unemployed or working for less than 16 hours a week, capable of and available for work for at least 40 hours a week and actively seeking a job. The applicant must also have entered into a Jobseeker's Agreement with an Employment Service adviser and must comply with any directions given. You may receive an occupational or personal pension of up to £50 a week before your contribution-based Jobseeker's Allowance is affected. Further information and a claim pack are available from local Jobcentres.

UNABLE TO WORK BECAUSE OF SICKNESS

Incapacity Benefit is available for someone unable to work through sickness or disability who has paid regular National Insurance contributions and is not receiving Statutory Sick Pay. The benefit is paid weekly and is not taxed for the first 28 weeks.

Application forms (Claim pack SSP1) for Incapacity Benefit should be provided by employers. Someone who is self-employed needs Claim Pack SC1, available from a doctor's surgery, hospital, Benefits Agency or Social Security office. Applications should be made within one month of the first day on which benefit is being claimed.

After 28 weeks, applicants claiming further benefit are expected to complete a question-naire and may be asked to have a medical examination to assess their capability for work.

Incapacity Benefit normally stops when a person reaches pensionable age and receives a State Retirement Pension. However, anyone previously on Invalidity Benefit who was over pensionable age on 13 April 1995, can continue to receive benefit up to the age of 65 for women and 70 for men.

Someone who has not paid enough National Insurance contributions to qualify for Incapacity Benefit may be able to claim *Severe*

Disablement Allowance. Applicants must generally be at least 80 per cent disabled and incapable of work for at least 28 weeks because of their sickness or disability. They must also be under 65 when they first qualify. More details are given in Social Security leaflet NI 252.

DISABLED AND IN WORK BUT WITH LIMITED EARNING CAPACITY

Disability working allowance is tax-free and available to people who do paid work for an average of 16 hours a week or more and are at a disadvantage in getting a job. The benefit is means-tested and there is a long list of qualifying requirements. Claims for Disability Working Allowance are made on form DWA1, available from Social Security offices and Jobcentres.

HELP WITH THE COSTS OF ILLNESS OR DISABILITY
Disability Living Allowance

A tax-free benefit for those who need help with getting around or with personal care. It is not affected by the value of a person's savings and is available to those

who are disabled and claim before their 65th birthday. Anyone claiming *after* reaching 65 should claim *Attendance Allowance* instead (see page 82).

Disability Living Allowance is given to people who need help, for example, with washing, dressing, using the toilet or perhaps preparing a cooked main meal. It may also be available to people who have a severe mental impairment, who have difficulty walking, or who need someone with them when they are out of doors.

The person must normally have been sufficiently ill or disabled for at least three months before the allowance can be paid, and the disability must be likely to continue for at least a further six months. Special rules apply to someone who has a terminal illness and is not expected to live longer than six months.

If you already receive a Disability Living Allowance and need to go into hospital as an in-patient, the Benefits Agency should be given the date of your admission. While you are in hospital you will continue to receive the Allowance for a period up to four weeks. If you remain in hospital longer than this, it will

BENEFITS

be discontinued. The Benefits Agency should be informed when you leave hospital, and your needs will then be reassessed.

If you go into a residential care or nursing home under arrangements made by Social Services, the care component of the Disability Living Allowance may stop after four weeks. It is important to inform the Benefits Agency when a person's circumstances change in this way.

Further information on the Disability Living Allowance is given in the Social Security leaflet DS704 or on the Benefit Enquiry Line, Freephone 0800 88 22 00. See **Contacts** for details.

Attendance Allowance

Available to people aged 65 or over, who need frequent help during the day or night with personal care, such as washing or eating.

To qualify for the Allowance, applicants must normally have needed care for at least six months before making the claim. Someone suffering from a terminal illness, who might not live longer than six months, can claim under special rules in order to obtain the benefit quickly. Attendance Allowance is tax-free and not affected by savings or (usually) income. It is also disregarded as income for Income Support claims.

The payment of Attendance Allowance, like Disability Living Allowance, may be affected if a person has to go into hospital or residential care. To get the right benefit, it is important to give the Benefits Agency or Social Security office the dates of admission and discharge.

Attendance Allowance can be claimed on form DS702, available from post offices, local Social Security and Benefit Agency offices.

Carers

If you are caring for a person who is sick or disabled and receiving Attendance Allowance or the middle or top rate of Disability Living Allowance care component, you may qualify for an *Invalid Care Allowance*.

This is available to someone who is:

• **not earning more than £50 a week after allowable expenses;**

• **not a paid professional, such as a doctor or nurse;**

• **providing care for at least 35 hours a week and for at least 22 weeks in every 26 week period; and**

• **not in full-time education.**

The Allowance is taxable but is not dependent on National Insurance contributions. More information on the Invalid Care Allowance is given in leaflet FB31 and claim pack DS700, available from local Social Security and Benefits Agency offices or via the Benefit Enquiry Line, see **Contacts** for details.

BENEFITS

BASIC LIVING EXPENSES
Income Support

Financial help for someone on a low income is available through Income Support. Eligibility is based on a number of factors, connected with both the applicant and their partner. These include their age, savings and income, whether they are employed, the number of hours they work each week, and whether there are people with special needs in the household.

As a very rough guide, in order to qualify for the benefit, the applicant and their partner must not have more than £8,000 in savings (or £16,000 for someone in a residential or nursing home), they should not be working 16 hours or more a week, their partner, if they have one, should not work 24 hours a week or more and their income should be below the qualifying level set each year by Parliament.

Income Support can be used to top up other benefits or earnings from part-time or self-employed work. It can also be paid to people who are being looked after by a carer and to the carers themselves, provided they meet the tests of eligibility.

A person on Income Support may qualify for other benefits such as housing benefit, free dental treatment and Council Tax Benefit.

Information and claim forms are available from local Benefits Agency or Social Security offices and the Citizens Advice Bureau. It is important to claim the benefit as soon as possible after becoming eligible. Payment of Income Support is not normally backdated.

The Benefits Agency Charter

The Benefits Agency Charter outlines the service you are entitled to receive from the Benefits Agency, and the procedure to follow should you need to make a complaint.

PAYMENTS FROM THE SOCIAL FUND

For more information on any of the following payments, contact your local Social Security or Benefits Agency office.

Community Care Grant

The grants are payable to people who receive (or are likely to be on leaving care) Income Support or income-based Jobseeker's Allowance. They are intended to help vulnerable people resettle in the community after institutional or residential care, or to remain in the community.

BENEFITS

Budgeting Loan

A loan of up to £1,000 can be provided for essential household equipment or other items. It is only available to someone who has been on Income Support or income-based Jobseeker's Allowance for at least 26 weeks. As it is a loan, it must be repaid over an agreed period of time.

Crisis Loan

An interest-free loan to help people in an emergency, or as a consequence of a disaster, where it is the only way of preventing serious damage or risk to health or safety. The loan is for specific items or living expenses and normally for a period not exceeding 14 days.

Cold Weather Payments

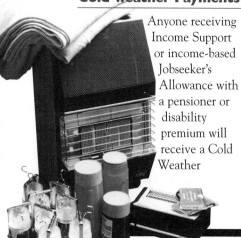

Anyone receiving Income Support or income-based Jobseeker's Allowance with a pensioner or disability premium will receive a Cold Weather Payment of £8.50 when the average temperature, for a period of seven consecutive days, has been recorded as, or is forecast to be, 0° Celsius or below. Payments are made automatically. There is no need to make a claim.

Winter Fuel Payments

In 1997, the Government announced that over the next two years all pensioners would be given help towards their fuel bills. All pensioner households are eligible to receive £20, with pensioners receiving Income Support entitled to £50.

HOUSING
Housing Benefit

A tax-free benefit providing help with rent and certain service charges to council, housing association and private tenants. To be eligible, applicants (with their partners) must have an income below a certain set level and savings of no more than £16,000. More information is provided with Income Support claim forms and in leaflets RR1 and RR2, available from Social Security and Benefit Agency offices. Further information is also obtainable from your local council.

Council Tax Benefit

The council tax system assigns domestic properties to one of eight valuation bands (the lowest being 'A' and the highest 'H'), depending on their estimated value in April 1991. One bill is sent to each self-contained dwelling and liability for the tax usually falls on those aged 18 or over, although members of the household can choose themselves how to divide up the bill.

People who live alone and single parents with children living at home are entitled to a reduction of 25 per cent in their council tax bill. Special reductions also apply to houses adapted for people with disabilities.

For people on a low income, help may be available through Council Tax Benefit. This is worked out on the basis of a person's income, savings and personal circumstances. Many people entitled to Income Support, Housing Benefit or Disability Working Allowance also qualify for Council Tax Benefit.

What is known as a **Second Adult Rebate** is available to householders who share their home with another adult who has a low income, does not pay council tax or rent and is not their partner. Someone who qualifies for Council Tax Benefit and Second Adult Rebate will receive the larger amount of the two.

More information is given in leaflet CTB 1, *Help with the council tax*, available from post offices and local Social Security offices.

benefits ha agency
An Executive Agency of the Department of Social Security

NI196 from April

Social security benefit rates

Benefit rates, earnings rules and National Insurance contributions rates

Benefit Rates

Benefit Rates

Benefit Rates

Be

CITIZENSHIP
FOUNDATION

BENEFITS

Fuel Debts

Most electricity and gas customers use their fuel before paying for it. The amount consumed is recorded by a credit meter, and bills are sent out at the end of each quarter.

Other alternatives include electricity and gas stamps (which can be bought at post offices and 'electricity shops'), installing a prepayment meter (using a card, which is slightly more expensive) or by paying by direct debit a your bank account. With this last option, the fuel company estimates the amount of fuel you will use in the coming year and, based on this, draws out an agreed amount of money each month from your bank account. If your electricity or gas consumption is below the estimate, you will receive a credit which can be carried over to the following year or repaid to you.

By law, all gas companies must provide free special help, if requested, to certain customers. These are people who are either pensioners, disabled or chronically sick and who live alone or with someone else who is of pensionable age, disabled or chronically sick or less than 18 years old.

The help available includes free safety checks, adapting gas appliances to make them easier to use, and moving the meter to a more convenient position. People who are blind or partially sighted can be provided with details of their meter readings and gas bill by telephone or other appropriate means.

Under normal circumstances, a gas company may cut off the supply to customers who do not pay their bills. However, if you are a pensioner who lives alone, or with other people who are pensioners or under 18 years of age, and you do not have enough money to pay your gas bill, the gas company will not disconnect your home between 1 October and 31 March. For further information, contact your gas supplier. Contact numbers for customers with special needs are given on the back of your gas bill.

BANKS

Most people today keep their money in a bank, building society or Post Office account. All have leaflets explaining their services and the different kinds of account they offer. Opening an account is quite straightforward. Although each bank and building society has its own procedure, they all require some form of identification and usually ask to see the applicant in person.

Tax on interest

Interest is taxed initially at 20%. However, anyone not paying tax (possibly because they only receive a State Pension or have a very low income) can ask their bank or building society to pay interest without tax deducted.

Ability to maintain an account

The production of a consistent signature and the mental capacity to understand the transactions being performed through the account are important elements of keeping a back account open.

If an account holder finds it difficult to produce a specific signature, arrangements can be made for some form of mark to represent his or her signature or for someone else to sign on their behalf. If it becomes evident that the account holder does not understand the transactions that are being made, then the account may be frozen.

However, this can be avoided if the account holder has completed an **enduring power of attorney**. This is a document which gives another person the right to manage the affairs of someone who has become mentally incapable of doing so (see page 88).

THE LONDON JOINT STOCK BANK LIMITED.

To prevent alterations and other forms of fraud in connection with Cheques, Customers are

FINANCIAL MATTERS

MANAGING ONE'S OWN AFFAIRS

The law provides some protection to those who can no longer cope properly with their financial affairs. There are two principal ways in which this achieved.

Enduring power of attorney

A document, signed and witnessed, in which one person (the *donor*) gives another (known as the *attorney*) the authority to act on their behalf, with regard to matters of finance and property. It is advisable to ask a solicitor to draw up the deed and arrange for it to be signed and witnessed in the correct way. The donor must understand what they are doing when they sign the deed. It is possible to appoint more than one attorney.

When the attorney suspects that the donor is becoming, or has become, mentally incapable of managing their affairs, he or she is required to inform certain relatives of the intention to apply to the Court of Protection for the enduring power of attorney to be registered. When this has been registered by the Court, the attorney can act on behalf of the donor with bodies such as banks and other commercial firms. Most powers of attorney are arranged when the

FINANCIAL MATTERS

INVESTMENTS

Many older people have money invested. A problem can occur when someone becomes mentally incapable. If this is the case, no further transactions can be made unless there is an **enduring power of attorney** and it has been registered. Income is received from investments in the form of dividends or interest payments. For tax purposes these may be paid with tax already deducted.

If this is the case, it is possible to claim back any overpaid tax at the end of the year.

donor is fit and well in order to provide for a time, at a later stage, when they might need such decisions made for them. Once registered, an enduring power of attorney can only be revoked by the court. It is terminated automatically by the death of the donor or the death, mental incapacity or bankruptcy of the attorney.

Court of Protection

When a person's mental capacity has deteriorated to the point where it is felt that they are incapable of managing their own financial affairs, a doctor, social worker, carer, member of their family etc. can apply to the Court of Protection to have the affairs of that person placed under the jurisdiction of the Court.

If the Court decides that there is sufficient medical evidence to show that the person is incapable of managing their affairs, it will appoint someone to act for them, such as a relative or the Director of Social Services. See **Contacts** for details.

INSURANCE

Insurance can provide compensation for an unexpected loss or mishap. It's possible to take out insurance against almost anything, including loss or damage to possessions, legal fees and unexpected veterinary bills. Insurance can be arranged by going direct to an insurance company or insurance *broker*.

Insurance companies who deal direct with the public by telephone are listed in Yellow Pages. They usually offer

CITIZENSHIP FOUNDATION

FINANCIAL MATTERS

competitive rates and can issue policies with the minimum of paperwork.

Insurance *brokers* act as agents to help the client choose an insurer and make the necessary arrangements. They don't charge for this, but make their money instead via commission from the insurance company the client decides to use.

It's a good idea to take time in deciding what the insurance covers and which policy is most suitable. It's also important to ask the sales advisor or broker about anything that is unclear. All the information you supply must be as accurate as possible. Not only should all the questions be answered truthfully, but other information that could be relevant should also be given. If it's not, the insurance policy may be invalid. It's also important to tell the insurance company of any change in your circumstances which may have a bearing on your policy.

Life Insurance

Life insurance provides a level of financial protection to members of a family, through a lump sum payment on the holder's death. It can be purchased in its own right, but is also sometimes available with company and personal pension schemes. Life insurance can be obtained from an appointed representative of an insurance company or an independent financial adviser. Some policies may be cashed in before death, although the amount received will be reduced.

Long-term care insurance

This type of insurance can cover part of the cost of staying in a nursing home or having a carer at home. Some life insurance policies offer long-term care as an additional benefit, although the majority do not. The premium payable depends upon your age, state of health and the type and level of benefits you choose.

TAX
Income tax

Everyone whose yearly income is above a certain level pays income tax. Employees have tax deducted each month or week directly from their salary or pay packet (PAYE). Self-employed people complete a tax return at the end of each tax year.

Most types of income are added together to determine the amount of tax a person must pay. However, tax is not paid on all sources of income. These include the following:
• Disability Living Allowance,
• Attendance Allowance,
• Incapacity Benefit paid to people who were previously receiving Invalidity Benefit and for new claimants for the first 28 weeks of Incapacity Benefit,
• Income Support,
• Council Tax Benefit,
• Housing Benefit,
• War Disablement and War Widow's Pension,
• proceeds from National Savings certificates and the first £70 income from a National Savings Ordinary Account.

When the only income a person receives is their State Pension, their income may well be lower than their personal tax allowance and they will probably not have to pay income tax. However, for someone with a personal or company pension, their State Pension is treated as taxable income and therefore uses up part of their personal tax allowance.

THE TAXPAYER'S CHARTER

The Taxpayer's Charter outlines the service you are entitled to expect from HM Customs and Excise.

BRITONS

YOUR COUNTRY WANTS YOUR MONEY

C☆TIZENSH☆P
FOUNDATION

FINANCIAL MATTERS

Allowances

Everyone resident in the UK for tax purposes is allowed a certain level of their income to be free of tax, known as a *personal tax allowance*. It is announced annually in the Budget. Currently (April 1998) the personal allowance is £4,195. Larger allowances are given to people aged 65 and over who have a gross income of less than £16,200 (April 1998).

Married couples receive an extra allowance, which again is raised when either partner reaches 65, with a further increase at 75. A husband and wife can jointly decide which of them shall be given the allowance or it can be claimed by both, and split between them. In the absence of a specific request, the allowance is normally given to the husband. A married couple who are not living together can still claim the *married couple's allowance* if neither of them wishes to make the separation permanent.

When a husband or wife dies, their widow or widower continues to receive the married couple's allowance for the remainder of the tax year in which the death occurred, less any part their partner used against their income. In addition, a widow will receive a *widow's bereavement allowance* during the year of her husband's death and the following year - unless she has remarried at the start of the second year.

In some circumstances, a couple may decide to switch savings from one person to another in order to make full use of each other's personal allowance. However transferring savings in this way may affect other benefits that the couple may receive.

The Inland Revenue publish many free leaflets on taxation, available from libraries, post offices and local tax offices. They also run a telephone helpline, see **Contacts** for details.

Tax and investment income

Income from savings and investments may be paid gross (without the deduction of tax) or with tax already deducted. Anyone receiving a gross payment is liable to pay tax on that amount, unless their total income falls below the tax thresholds. Equally, someone receiving payments with tax deducted may be able to claim back any overpaid tax, using form R40.

Savings income is treated as the top slice of your income. However, in order to encourage people to save, there is a tax rate of 20% for both low and basic rate taxpayers. A higher rate taxpayer pays 40% tax on savings income. If your savings income pushes you from the basic rate to the higher rate, the income is apportioned between the two rates and taxed partly at 20% and partly at 40%.

Bank and building society interest

Interest may be paid with or without a deduction of 20% in tax. If you expect not to have to pay tax because your total income will be less than your *personal tax allowance* (see above), you can register to have interest paid without tax deducted, using form R85, available from banks, building societies and post offices.

Capital gains tax

This is a tax on the gain in value of an asset during the time the taxpayer has owned it. The tax is levied when the item is sold or given away or disposed of in any other way. The gain is taxed at the rate of the taxpayer's top slice of income. There is a tax-free allowance or threshold for individual taxpayers of £6,800 (April 1998), updated annually.

Gains on the disposal of certain assets, such as a person's main dwelling house and savings certificates are exempt from capital gains tax, as is the transfer of capital assets between husband and wife - unless the partner who received the assets later decides to sell them to someone else.

Tax relief is also possible for someone, aged 50 or over, who disposes of their business or is forced to retire because of ill health. The level of tax relief, called *retirement relief*, depends on the size of the gain and the length of time they owned the business or held the full-time directorship.

CITIZENSHIP FOUNDATION

FINANCIAL MATTERS

Inheritance tax

This is a tax on the value of a person's assets at death and gifts made seven years before death. The tax bill may be reduced for those gifts were made three years or more before death. Essentially, if you give away property or possessions before you die, there will usually be no inheritance tax on those assets.

A number of other gifts are exempt from inheritance tax: that is gifts totalling up to £3,000 in each tax year, plus any unused balance of the £3,000 from the previous tax year; gifts of £250 or less to any one person and wedding gifts - up to £5,000 by each parent or step-parent; £2,500 by each grandparent or great-grandparent or by either party to the marriage; or £1,000 by people outside these categories. There are other exemptions for gifts made to UK charities, political parties housing associations or for UK 'national purposes' e.g. to a museum or university. Any transfer made between husbands and wives is usually exempt from tax.

Wills

Usually tax must be paid before probate or administration is granted, and the personal representatives may find that a bank or building society is unwilling to release money held in the deceased's account. In such cases it may be necessary to raise a loan to pay the tax bill and probate court fees. Once probate has been granted, the loan can be repaid from released funds.

The sale of assets from the estate by the personal representatives, in order to raise money to pay debts and funeral and testamentary expenses, is normally inevitable where there is not enough cash in the deceased's bank or building society account to cover such charges. For more information on what to do when someone dies, see pages 30 - 38.

WILLS
and
TRUSTS

There are advantages in appointing the Bank as Executor or Trustee.
▪
The utmost secrecy is assured.
▪
NATIONAL

TRAVEL
& TRANSPORT

PUBLIC TRANSPORT

FARES AND TICKETS

DRIVING

ACCIDENTS

BUYING A CAR

CYCLING

BUSES AND LONDON UNDERGROUND

When you pay for a bus fare, you enter into a contract with the bus company - but it doesn't actually begin until you buy your ticket. This means that if the bus arrives late, or doesn't come at all, there is little you can do other than complain to the company operating the service. If you are not satisfied with the answer you receive or the service provided, you can complain to the local Traffic Commissioner. The Citizens Advice Bureau can give you the address.

If you have a comment or complaint about the service on a *London* bus route, you can write to the operator whose address is shown on every bus. If you are not satisfied with the reply, contact London Transport Buses who are responsible for providing bus services in London. Should you still remain dissatisfied, you may wish to take up your concerns with the London Regional

Passengers' Committee, the consumer watchdog body set up by Parliament

to investigate passengers' complaints. See **Contacts** for further details.

The majority of bus services outside London are run, on a commercial basis, by private operators who are free to operate where they choose, subject to certain registration requirements. Under the *Transport Act 1985*, Passenger Transport Authorities and county councils have a duty to ensure that an "appropriate" level of service is provided, which particularly takes account of the needs of elderly and disabled people.

Problems with Underground services in London should first be addressed to the Customer Service Centre, London Under-ground and then, if you are still not satisfied, to the London Regional Passengers' Committee. Addresses and telephone numbers of both organisations are given in the **Contacts** section.

London Transport Buses and London Underground both have Charters outlining the standard of service they aim to provide and how to complain if things go wrong. They undertake to give full written replies to complaints within three weeks of receipt. Copies of the Charters are available from their Customer Service Centres.

TRAINS

When you travel on a train you enter into a contract with the train operating company, but again your ticket gives no legal guarantee that the train will run on time (or even at all) or that you'll have a seat when it does come. All this is explained in the leaflet, known as the conditions of carriage, available free of charge from station ticket offices.

Each train operating company has its own *Passenger's Charter* outlining the standard of service it aims to provide and explaining the circumstances in which compensation may be given. If you wish to complain about a train service, write to the customer relations manager for the route you have travelled on. Forms are available from main line stations. If you are not satisfied with the response, you can contact your local Rail User's Consultative Committee (in London it is the London Regional Passengers'

Committee), enclosing all correspondence you've had with the train operator. If you remain dissatisfied, take your complaint to the Rail Regulator. See **Contacts** for details.

Fares and tickets

If the standard class is full, you have no right to sit, or even stand, in the first class section, without prior permission from the on-train staff. If this has not been given, the inspector is entitled to ask you to move or pay the difference between the first and standard class fare.

If you travel on a train or London Underground without a ticket, you are, in law, a trespasser and may be asked to pay the full fare or leave details of your name and address. On some train services and all Underground Railway routes you may also be charged an on-the-spot penalty. Information about this is displayed at stations where the system is in operation.

If you are stranded at a station without any money for a ticket, your ticket can be bought for you by someone else at another station, with the authorisation sent by telephone to where you are waiting. This is known as a *silk arrangement*.

GETTING ABOUT

COACH TRAVEL

Recent changes in the law mean that most coaches are now banned from the outside lane of a motorway and are fitted with 65mph speed limiters. All new designs of coach must now include seat belts, as must all coaches registered after 1 October 1999.

CONCESSIONS
Buses

Bus passes, which may also extend to local trains and the Underground, entitling older people to free travel or lower fares are available in most parts of the country. Schemes vary from place to place and local councils don't *have* to offer these concessions.

Women normally qualify at 60 and men at 65, but a few local authorities have set higher age limits of 65 or even 70. Men and women are treated differently because the concessions are based on *state* pension age, which will be equalised over a period between 2010 - 2020.

More information on travel passes is obtainable from your local authority and from London Transport or Passenger Transport Executive enquiry offices.

Cheap or free bus travel is available for blind and disabled people in many areas. Your local council will have information.

Trains

A *Senior Railcard*, costing £18, allows a third off most rail fares and is available to people aged 60 or over. Savings are also available with a *Rail Europ Senior Card*, which costs a further £5. Application forms may be obtained from local main line stations and rail appointed travel agents. Concessions are available for all passengers aged 60 or over on *Eurostar* services.

A *Disabled Persons Railcard* gives a third off most rail fares and

TRAVEL & TRANSPORT

allows the holder to take a companion at the same reduced rate. The card costs £14 and is valid for 12 months. The leaflet Rail Travel for Disabled Passengers gives further details and is available from main line stations.

Disabled people in wheelchairs who do not hold a railcard can also get reductions on full fare single and open return tickets, with the same rates also applying to a companion.

Coaches

Advantage 50, a discount coachcard for the over 50s, costs £8 a year and £19 for three years, and gives 30% off many fares with National Express.

STAN IS STUNNED

Euro Court says "Too young for Bus Pass"

Stanley Atkins applied to his local council for a bus pass. The council's policy was to issue bus passes to women and men when they reached retire-ment age - at 60 and 65 respectively. Stanley, 63, was told that he was too young and his request for a pass was turned down. He felt this was unfair and took his case to court to retrieve the money he had to pay in extra bus fares. Although different retirement ages for men and women are quite legal, Stanley argued that allocating bus passes on this basis was contrary to European sex discrimination law, which forbids unfair treatment on matters of health and social assistance. Stanley stressed that access to cheap transport was socially very important for older people.

Five years later, in 1996, his case reached the European Court. The judges decided that cheap or free bus fares did not qualify as a social or health benefit and that Stanley's local council were therefore not breaking European sex discrimination law. Stanley lost his case and, in most places, men still have to wait longer than women to qualify for certain travel concessions.

Travel Permit
Elderly or Disabled Persons
Expires:
HALF RATE TRAVEL

SENIOR RAILCARD

Rail Travel for Disabled Passengers

50 OR OVER SAVE UP TO 30% WITH THE NEW *Advantage 50*

TAXIS
Licenced taxis

The only vehicles licensed to wait in a taxi rank or stop for passengers who hail them in the street. The vehicles must be checked regularly and fares are normally set by the licensing authority.

Under the *Disability Discrimination Act 1995*, newly licensed (and eventually all) taxis will have to be fully accessible to disabled travellers. Taxi drivers will be required to help disabled people in and out of taxis and to help with their luggage. They will also be expected to carry guide and hearing dogs free of charge.

Private hire cars or minicabs

These must be booked in advance or ordered, in person, from the cab office. Minicab drivers are forbidden by law to ply for hire by waiting at a taxi rank or by picking up on the street. If you do succeed in flagging one down you may not be covered by insurance if there's a crash. It's advisable to agree the fare before you set off. Minicabs and private hire cars will be generally unaffected by the *Disability Discrimination Act.*

DISABLED TRAVELLERS

The *Disability Discrimination Act 1995* is designed to reduce discrimination faced by many disabled people. Under the Act, the Government will make regulations aiming to ensure that disabled people can get on and off public transport in safety and without too much difficulty. All trains and trams brought into service after 31 December 1998 must be accessible to disabled people. Train operators will also give help to disabled people if they are given notice of their intention to travel. Further details of the service offered to disabled people can be found in the Charters issued by each operator.

DISABILITY LIVING ALLOWANCE

The Disability Living Allowance (DLA) is available for severely disabled people under the age of 65. It has two parts - a care and a mobility component. Either or both components may be awarded, depending on the effect of the disability. The mobility component is available to disabled people who are unable or virtually unable to walk, or who need someone with them when walking outdoors. Receipt of the higher rate of the mobility component provides access to the Motability Scheme. Once awarded, the DLA is available for as long as the disabled person continues to meet the entitlement criteria. There are no upper age limits, but applications must be made before the age of 65 is reached. Forms are available from Benefit Agency offices.

THE LICENCE

It is an offence to drive a vehicle without the correct licence. Learner drivers need a provisional licence. Car drivers can hold the same provisional licence until they are 70. A motorcyclist's provisional licence is only valid for two years and cannot be renewed for a further 12 months after this. Application forms for all licences are available from a post office.

Your full driving licence is normally valid until you reach the age of 70. Shortly before your seventieth birthday, the licensing centre (DVLA, Swansea) will send you a reminder for renewal. It will include an application form for a new licence and a health questionnaire for you (not your doctor) to complete. If the licensing centre is satisfied that you are still fit enough to drive, a new licence will be issued, renewable every three years, for a fee of £6.

If you have any health problems which may affect your ability to drive, it is your responsibility (and not your doctor's) to inform the DVLA. Failure to do this is a criminal offence, under the *Road Traffic Act 1988*. If your doctor believes you are unfit to drive, he or she should explain why and encourage you to inform the licensing centre. If you refuse, the doctor can - though breaking patient confidentiality -write to the DVLA, expressing his or her concerns.

If you are refused a licence, you can appeal against the decision at the magistrates' court. However, the DVLA will bring medical evidence and instruct a lawyer to present their case - which means that, if you lose, you could be faced with a large bill for costs.

C*TIZENSH*P
FOUNDATION

CARS & MOTORCYCLES

MOT

Most vehicles of three or more years old must pass the MOT test if they are to be used on the road.

INSURANCE

It is an offence to drive, ride or even park a motor vehicle on the road without insurance, even if you made a mistake by genuinely believing that you were insured. Failure to have insurance means a fine and penalty points on a licence, and possible disqualification.

It is also an offence to allow your car or motorcycle to be used by a person who is not insured to drive it.

There are three different kinds of motor insurance, offering different levels of cover:

• *third party insurance* only pays for damage caused to other people or their property. This is the minimum level of insurance cover required by law;

• *third party fire and theft* gives you further protection by covering you against theft or fire damage to your own vehicle;

• *comprehensive insurance* is usually the most expensive, but covers the cost of accident repair damage to your own vehicle, as well as compensating others for injuries or damage in the accident.

If you tow a caravan or trailer, your normal car insurance will provide third party cover. However, you'll need a separate policy, or an extension of the existing one, if you want to cover the caravan or trailer

ROAD TAX

A car or motorbike which is being used, or just allowed to stand on the road, must display a current tax disc. Failure to tax a vehicle can mean a fine of up to £1,000 or five times the annual rate of excise duty for the vehicle, whichever is the greater. A person who buys a disc, but fails to display it, also commits an offence. The DVLA can authorise any vehicle not displaying a valid tax disc to be wheelclamped or impounded.

It's often said that drivers have 14 days to renew a tax disc after it has expired. This is not correct. There is no period of grace in law. However it is common practice to allow motorists 14 days grace to apply for and obtain a new licence. Owners who decide not to use or keep their vehicle on the public road must now inform the DVLA. Details of this are sent with the licence reminders.

Owners of cars over 25 years old or vehicles used by, or for the sole use of, disabled passengers in receipt of certain DSS benefits must licence their vehicles in the usual way but do not have to pay for their disc. More information is available from the DVLA (Driving and Vehicle Licensing Agency), see **Contacts**.

CARS & MOTORCYCLES

against loss or damage.

When you apply for insurance, the information you give must be accurate. If it's not, and you knew it was not accurate, your insurers can make your insurance invalid and avoid any claims that have been made. It is an offence knowingly to make a false statement to obtain insurance.

Sarah bought a Morgan sports car, and insured it for her and her fiancé to drive. The car, worth £26,000, was stolen. When she claimed on her insurance, it came to light that another car of Sarah's had been stolen several years ago, and she had failed to mention this on the application form. The insurance policy was not valid, and Sarah received no compensation for the loss of her car.

ACCIDENTS

If you are involved in an accident...

• **Stop immediately.** It's an offence to drive away without stopping.

• **Check that everyone involved in the accident is OK.** If anyone is injured, call an ambulance before you do anything else.

• **You must give your name and address and details of your vehicle to anyone who has reasonable need to know them.** This includes a police officer attending the scene of the accident, anyone whose vehicle or property is damaged, a witness to the accident and the owner of any animal injured or killed. (This applies to horses, cows, sheep, goats, dogs - but not cats.) You must also produce your insurance certificate, or evidence that you are insured, if someone is injured. If you are unable to do this at the time of the accident, then you must give this information to the police as soon as is reasonably practicable and certainly within 24 hours. If you don't, you will be committing an offence. If the police attend the accident,

CARS & MOTORCYCLES

make a note of the officer's number.

• **As soon as you can, write down everything that happened.** This should cover time of day, weather, light, estimated speeds, position of vehicles before and after the accident, what people said and anything else that you think might be relevant. If you can, take photos before anything is moved or draw a sketch plan as soon as you feel able to do so.

• **Be cautious if the other driver suggests not calling the police and offers you cash to cover the damage.** It might be an offence not to report the accident, and you may find that the damage to your vehicle costs a lot more than you are being offered.

• **Don't admit it was your fault.** You may find later that the other driver was drunk, driving too fast or without lights - in which case you might not be to blame at all. If you do admit responsibility, your words may end up by being used against you in court and may affect your insurance claim.

• **Contact your insurance company as soon as possible.**

Accidents: When to call the police

There is no need to call the police as long as the driver has given his or her name, address and car registration number to anyone who has reasonable grounds for knowing them (see above).

If someone is injured in the accident, a driver must also show his or her actual certificate of insurance to anyone who has reasonable grounds to see it. If this is not possible, the driver must report the accident to the police as soon as possible and certainly within 24 hours.

Injuries

If you are injured - as a passenger or driver - through the fault of someone else, you may be entitled to compensation. Get in touch with a solicitor as soon as you can. An initial interview will probably cost very little and, in some cases, nothing at all. It will give you a good idea of what you should do next but, before you proceed much further, check what the overall costs are likely to be.

CARS & MOTORCYCLES

No insurance

If you are a victim of a hit-and-run driver, or have an accident with someone who is uninsured, get in touch with the *Motor Insurance Bureau* (see **Contacts**). The MIB is funded by the insurance industry and was set up to help the victims of untraced and uninsured motorists. These matters can be complicated, so again it is worth consulting a solicitor for guidance.

> **Peter was involved in a crash with a motor cycle. He feared that it was his fault and that he would lose his licence, as he already had a number of penalty points. He persuaded his wife Sophie, who was not in the car at the time, to tell the police that it was she who was driving. A week later they both admitted the deception, but were charged with perverting the course of justice. Peter and Sophie were sentenced to four and two months in prison.**

SEATBELTS AND CRASH HELMETS

Drivers and both front and rear seat passengers must now wear seat belts where they are fitted. If a passenger in your car does not wear a belt, he or she may be prosecuted - unless that passenger is a child under 14, when it is your responsibility to see that a seat belt is worn.

Front and rear seat belts have had to be fitted to all new cars since 1987. You do not have to have seat belts fitted to an older car without them.

Someone injured in an accident, who was not wearing a seat belt, would probably be judged to have contributed to their own injuries. Any damages they might be awarded would therefore be significantly reduced.

Motorcyclists and pillion passengers must wear approved safety helmets on all journeys. This regulation does not apply to a follower of the Sikh religion while he is wearing a turban.

CITIZENSHIP FOUNDATION

CARS & MOTORCYCLES

SPEEDING

Breaking the speed limit is an *absolute* offence, which means that it is no defence to say that you were not causing any danger, or that you didn't realise that you were travelling so fast.

If you break the speed limit or are seen by the police to be driving carelessly or dangerously, they must warn you of the possibility of prosecution at the time of the offence or serve you with a summons within 14 days of the offence. Otherwise you cannot be

convicted, unless an accident occurred at the time, or immediately after, the incident in question.

60

Motorways and trunk roads

The Highways Agency and the Transport and Highways Directorate in Wales maintain the countries' motorways and trunk roads. For information on roadworks, trunk roads and motorways, tel. 0345 50 40 30 (England) and 01 222 825 111 (Wales). The Road User's Charter is available from the Highways Agency, tel 0345 50 40 30.

The Highways Agency also publish *Your Home and Trunk Road Proposals*, explaining the procedures involved in making proposals for new trunk roads, public consultation and paying compensation to people whose homes are affected by these schemes.

Speed limits

30

50

Speed limits depend on the type of road and the vehicle.

Cars and motorcycles:

Built up areas	30 mph*
Single carriageways	60 mph
Dual carriageways	70 mph
Motorways	70 mph

Cars with a trailer/caravan:

Built up areas	30 mph*
Single carriageways	50 mph
Dual carriageways	60 mph
Motorways	60 mph

* The 30mph limit applies to all traffic on all roads with street lighting, unless road signs show otherwise.

70

DRIVING OFFENCES

Careless driving is driving in a way which is not how a careful and reasonable driver would behave. Pulling out from a side road without looking is an example of this.

Dangerous driving is driving in a way which is dangerous to people or property, such as

CARS & MOTORCYCLES

driving very fast through a built up area, or overtaking on a sharp bend. Dangerous driving and causing death by dangerous driving are extremely serious offences, which courts will nowadays punish with fines, disqualification and possibly imprisonment. If you face such a charge, get in touch with a solicitor straightaway.

DRINKING AND DRIVING

The law does not limit drivers to a certain number of drinks, but does specify the maximum amount of alcohol you may have in your body while driving or being in charge of a vehicle. In law, this includes simply sitting in the driving seat of a parked car.

Alcohol - the limits

Alcohol in the body can be measured in the breath, blood or urine. A driver will be found guilty of drink-driving if he or she has more than 35 micrograms of alcohol in 100 millilitres of breath, 80 milligrams of alcohol in 100 millilitres of blood, or more than 107 milligrams of alcohol in 100 millilitres of urine. In 1999 or 2000, it is likely that the permitted level of alcohol a driver may consume will be further reduced.

Breath tests

The police can breathalyse anyone whom they reasonably suspect of driving with excess alcohol, who is committing a moving traffic offence, or has been involved in a road accident, however minor, even if there is no suspicion of alcohol.

If the test is positive, the driver will be arrested and taken to a police station for further tests. These will produce an exact reading of the breath alcohol level for evidence, should the driver be prosecuted. A sample of blood, or occasionally urine, may be required when a breath testing instrument is not available; or the instrument indicates that it cannot finalise a breath alcohol reading; or a police officer has reasonable cause to believe that there are medical reasons why the driver cannot provide a sample; or a police surgeon considers that the driver may be under the influence of drugs.

Courts rarely accept that there are special reasons for drivers

being over the limit.
Disqualification from driving is
almost always automatic. A
drunken driver who causes
someone's death may be sent to
prison for up to ten years and
disqualified from driving. A
driver who refuses to give a
breath sample commits an
offence and, if found guilty, will
almost certainly still end up with
a heavy fine and disqualification
from driving.

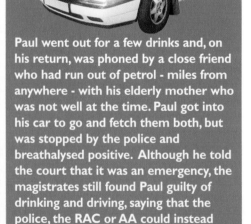

**Paul went out for a few drinks and, on
his return, was phoned by a close friend
who had run out of petrol - miles from
anywhere - with his elderly mother who
was not well at the time. Paul got into
his car to go and fetch them both, but
was stopped by the police and
breathalysed positive. Although he told
the court that it was an emergency, the
magistrates still found Paul guilty of
drinking and driving, saying that the
police, the RAC or AA could instead
have been called to help.**

PENALTY POINTS

Courts deal with most motoring
offences through a system of
penalty points, which are written
on a driver's licence. Anyone
receiving twelve or more points
with-in a period of three years
will almost always be disqualified
from driving for at least six
months. Details of the points
carried by each offence are given
in the Highway Code.

BUYING A CAR
New

Under the *Sale of Goods
Act 1979*, a new car
should be of *satisfactory
quality, fit for its purpose* and
as described, in addition to
further cover given by the
manufacturer's warranty. (These
terms are explained in more
detail on page 114.)

If you are not happy with a
new (or second-hand) car,
contact the dealer immediately,
put your complaint in writing,
and return the car. If the
problem is not sorted out to
your satisfaction, you may get
some help from the
manufacturer or the trade
association to which the dealer
belongs.

CARS & MOTORCYCLES

Second-hand

A car bought privately is usually cheaper than one purchased from a dealer, but you have fewer rights if things go wrong. The legal expression *"caveat emptor"*, meaning *"buyer beware"*, particularly applies to second-hand cars. It is notoriously difficult to get problems sorted out once you have paid your money.

If you buy from a dealer you are protected by the *Sale of Goods Act 1979*, which means it should be *of satisfactory quality, fit for its purpose* and *as described*.

A car bought privately need only be *as described*. You may find that none of these rights apply to cars sold at an auction if the seller issues a disclaimer saying "sold as seen."

• Look at the car in daylight. Take along someone who knows about cars. For between £100-£300 the RAC, AA or Green Flag will inspect and report on the mechanical state of the car, check to see if hire-purchase payments are still owed and whether the car has been stolen or is a write-off. HPI Autodata or AA Car Data provide a similar service at slightly lower cost, without the mechanical

inspection.

• Look to see if the car's mileage tallies with the MOT certificate and service history. You

can also check with previous owners. Ask the dealer if they have tried to verify the mileage. Be wary if there is a sticker on the speedometer indicating that there is no guarantee that the mileage is accurate.

• Ask to see the **Vehicle Registration Document** (V5). If it's a private sale, it should contain the seller's name and address. It also gives the **Vehicle Identification Number** (VIN), which should correspond with the number stamped on identi-fication plates under the bonnet and on the floor. If you have any worries, leave the car alone.

• If you buy a car which turns out to be stolen, it remains the property of the true owner. This means that you will almost certainly lose your money, unless you can get it back from the person from whom you bought the car.

CARS & MOTORCYCLES

Anna went to look at a Ford Escort, advertised privately in her local paper. She asked the seller if the car had been in an accident, he said no. Later, having bought the car, Anna found evidence of major crash repairs. She went back to the seller, pointed out the car was not as described and eventually got her money back. However, if the car had just been unreliable (even breaking down on the way back to her house), there is probably little she could have done, as there is nothing in law that states that a car bought privately must be of satisfactory or reasonable quality.

days are shown on the signs, the restrictions are in force everyday, including Sundays and Bank Holidays.

It is an offence to park in a way that endangers other road users, obscures a driver's view of the road, or causes any kind of obstruction. This is explained further in the Highway Code.

At night, vehicles should be parked facing in the direction of traffic flow.

Clamping

The law surrounding the right of private landowners to clamp vehicles parked on their land is not clear, although courts have judged this to be acceptable where the landowner has warned of the possibility of clamping and not charged an exorbitant fee for release. In these circumstances, a car owner who broke a clamp to free his car was ordered by the court to pay for the damage to the clamp. The government is looking at ways of regulating the use of clamps and plans to draw up a code of practice.

PARKING

Parking is always restricted in areas marked with yellow or red lines. The times at which restrictions apply are shown on nearby plates or on entry signs to controlled parking zones. If no

CARS & MOTORCYCLES

Orange badges

Badge holders may park free of charge and without a time limit:
• at parking meters and "pay and display" on-street parking;
• where others may park only for a limited time;
• on single or double yellow lines for up to three hours, except where there is a ban on loading and unloading.

If you qualify for an Orange Badge you can use it in any vehicle in which you travel - as either driver or passenger. However, it is an offence to allow anyone else to use the badge. If this occurs, the person using the badge may be fined up to £1,000 and the holder may have the badge withdrawn.

Badges are available through local authorities (usually social services). They can be used throughout Great Britain (although not in parts of central London and certain other town centres, where they have their own scheme for residents) and most west European countries. Applicants may be given a medical form for completion by a doctor and eligibility largely depends on a person's ability to walk - although badges can also be given to registered blind people and to people with disabilities in their upper limbs. Orange Badges are automatically available to people who receive the higher rate mobility component of the Disability Living Allowance or war pensioner's mobility supplement.

There are restrictions on where badge-holders can park. It is an offence to park causing an obstruction or danger to other vehicles or road users, eg close to a junction, in spaces or lanes for other vehicles, such as taxis or buses, and where there are double white lines, even if one of them is broken.

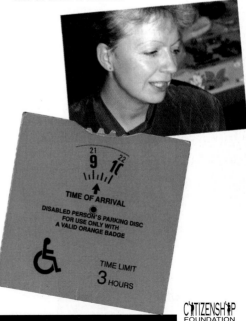

21 22
9 10
TIME OF ARRIVAL
DISABLED PERSON'S PARKING DISC
FOR USE ONLY WITH
A VALID ORANGE BADGE

TIME LIMIT
3 HOURS

CITIZENSHIP
FOUNDATION

CYCLING

Cyclists have to obey the same basic laws as all road users. They have a duty of care to pedestrians and other riders and drivers and must ensure that their bicycle is in roadworthy condition. It is an offence to ride under the influence of alcohol, although a police officer cannot breathalyse a cyclist, as motorists' drink and drive limits do not apply to cyclists. A court would instead be guided by the evidence of the arresting officer.

It is an offence to leave a bike in a dangerous position or on a clearway as it is to wheel a bike past a red traffic light or ride across a zebra crossing.

It is also against the law, under the *Highways Act 1835*, to ride a bicycle (or tricycle) on the pavement. In this matter, however, the police often use their discretion and accept that many cyclists, particularly younger children, choose not to ride in the road because of the traffic. However, if they feel it is necessary, the police will issue a verbal warning or take stronger action.

If an accident (or damage to a car) is caused by a child, the parent or guardian is not

normally liable in law - unless it can be shown that the parent was negligent in some way or that the child was acting on the parent's instruction or acting as an agent for the parent - for example by going on an errand.

GOODS
& SERVICES

CONSUMER RIGHTS

GUARANTEES

MAIL ORDER

UNFAIR CONTRACTS

CREDIT AND H.P.

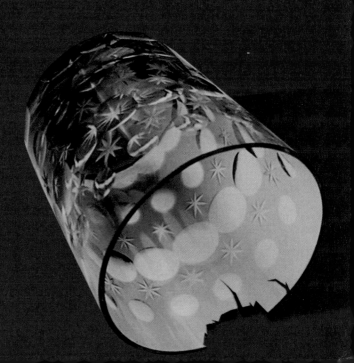

When you buy goods or services, you make a contract with the shop or person you are dealing with. Many of the customer's rights in this contract are set out in the *Sale of Goods Act 1979* and the *Supply of Goods and Services Act 1982*.

as described

The goods must fit the description on the packaging, the advertisement, or what was said at the time of sale. A scarf described as pure silk, must be just that.

GOODS

Under the *Sale of Goods Act 1979*, which was amended in 1994, items from a shop or trader (but not a private sale), must be...

of satisfactory quality

The customer can expect them to be free of faults and not scratched or damaged. This equally applies to goods bought in a sale.

However this does not apply if the fault was pointed out by the sales assistant or the customer had a good opportunity to discover the fault before making the purchase.

Second-hand goods bought from a shop or trader must also be of satisfactory quality, taking into account that they will probably not be in the same condition as they would have been, if new.

fit for all their intended purposes

This means that they must do what the seller, packaging or advertisements claim, and this includes any purpose mentioned by you to the seller. If the manufacturer or sales assistant states that an adhesive will bond plastic and metal and it doesn't, then it is not fit for its intended purpose.

You are less protected in law when buying goods *privately*, rather than from a shop or a trader. Goods bought privately need only be as described.

GOODS AND SERVICES

Presents

Strictly speaking, the only person entitled to a refund on a faulty present is the person who bought it - because it was she or he who entered into a contract with the shopkeeper, not the person to whom it was given. Therefore, if you buy someone a present it's a good idea to keep the receipt to pass on to them, in the event of a problem with the goods.

Mail order

Your legal rights are the same buying goods through the post as they are from a shop. If the goods are faulty, you are entitled to your money back, and the return postage costs. Although there is no legal requirement that the goods you order should arrive within a certain time, the delivery period should not be "unreasonable". If time is important, explain this to the company when you order. In this way you clearly make it part of the contract.

If you pay by credit card, you have more protection, although this only applies to goods costing £100 or more. (Some credit card companies now have a limit of £50.) If there is a problem with what you have bought you can claim against the credit card company as well as the seller, which is useful if the seller goes out of business.

You have further security if an advert in a newspaper or magazine carries the *Mail Order Protection Scheme* or *Periodical Publishers Association* logos. If the company you place your order with goes into liquidation before you receive the goods, your money should be protected.

Guarantees

These offer extra protection, on top of other legal rights. If there is a problem with something you have bought, it is usually better to report the matter to the retailer, with whom you made the contract. However, if the firm has gone out of business or the goods were bought abroad, making it difficult to return them, it may be worth claiming on the guarantee via the manufacturer.

CITIZENSHIP
FOUNDATION

CONTRACTS

Every time you buy something from a shop, or pay for a service, a legal agreement is made - known, in law, as a contract.

Contracts can be spoken as well as written and, in some circumstances, not even words are required. A contract is still made when the customer silently hands the money to a shopkeeper in payment for a bar of chocolate selected from the display.

In a contract both sides agree to give something of value to the other and to make the agreement legally binding. The contract is usually made when the shopkeeper agrees to provide certain goods in return for the money paid by the customer. Contracts for the purchase of items in a supermarket are made when the cashier rings them up on the till and by mail order when the order is made over the telephone or the order form placed in the post box.

Technically speaking, once a contract has been formed, it may only be changed with the agreement of both parties. However, some shops do allow customers to exchange unwanted items or provide a refund if the goods are returned in mint condition with the receipt. They don't have to do this by law.

Unfair contracts

If you find yourself tied to a contract which appears unfair or unreasonable, there are two pieces of legislation which may offer some protection.

Under the *Unfair Contract Terms Act 1977*, consumers are not held to the terms of a contract that unreasonably attempts to limit or exclude the trader's liability. For example, a company installing burglar alarms might include a clause in the contract stating it will not be responsible if the alarm fails when a burglar breaks in. This is unreasonable and is unlikely to be upheld in law.

The *Unfair Terms in Consumer Contracts Regulations 1994* state that the standard terms of a consumer contract must be fair. If they are not, they will not be binding on the consumer. For example the terms of a contract which gives the company the right to raise the price without the consumer having the right to cancel would be considered unfair. The Regulations also require the contract to be written in plain intelligible language. If it's not, it may be regarded as unfair.

If you are tied by a term or condition in a consumer contract which you feel is unfair contact your local Citizen's Advice Bureau, consumer advice centre or the Office of Fair Trading (see **Contacts**) which has a duty to investigate complaints over unfair contract terms.

Understanding what's happening

Sometimes a situation can arise in which a contract is made by a person who does not have the mental capacity to understand the implications of what they are doing. Obviously this can be complicated and is something over which legal advice should be taken. However, broadly speaking, the contract is likely to stand unless it can be shown that, for example, the shopkeeper or sales person knew or should have been aware of the customer's incapacity.

SERVICES

Dry cleaners, shoe repairers, mechanics and anyone else providing a service for a customer are governed by the *Supply of Goods and Services Act 1982*. This states that services should be provided…

with reasonable care and skill

within a reasonable time and

for a reasonable charge, when no price is agreed in advance

The person who carries out the service should do so with the skill of a competent member of that trade or profession - although this can be difficult to judge. If a plumber, for example, is called to do a repair and does not cure the fault, it is not a reason for the customer to refuse to pay. The customer is obliged to pay a reasonable amount for the service - assuming the plumber did not act in an incompetent way.

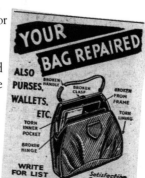

YOUR BAG REPAIRED

ALSO PURSES, WALLETS, ETC.

BROKEN HANDLE
BROKEN CLASP
BROKEN FROM FRAME
TORN INNER POCKET
TORN LINING
BROKEN HINGE

WRITE FOR LIST

Satisfaction Guaranteed

SERVICES

Sometimes a service is undertaken without agreement on overall price. Where the price is not agreed in advance, it is an implied term of the contract that a *reasonable* rate will be charged. If you feel you have been overcharged, it is worth seeking a reduction by explaining why you feel as you do. It is unwise to refuse to pay the charge. You can, however, pay the full amount under protest (putting this in writing) and then seek a refund by complaining to the company perhaps with the support of a second opinion (preferably written) from another tradesperson. Court action is a last resort and it is important first to seek legal advice, (see page 168).

Problems are less likely to occur if certain things can be agreed before the work is started - such as the cost, the time it will take and what will happen if, for example, the item can't be repaired.

The Citizens Advice Bureau or local consumer advice department can advise on how to deal with a problem over a service and how far it may be worth taking a complaint. They can also tell you whether other people have reported similar problems with the same trades person or company.

Some trades and professional bodies have a code of practice which members are expected to follow. These have no legal standing but they can provide a means of dealing with a customer's complaint in a reasonable way. The Citizens Advice Bureau or consumer advice department will have contact details.

PUT DOWNS

Some shops will do as much as they can to help you deal with a problem over something you have bought. Others may try to put you off and not live up to their legal obligations.

"We'll send it back to the workshop"

Only if you want them to. If the fault appears shortly after you buy the goods, and you haven't misused them, you need not face further inconvenience by having them repaired. You are entitled to your money back.

If the item worked well at first and then developed a fault, you may still be entitled to some or all of your money back, to be offered a replacement or to have it repaired free of charge. It all depends on how long you have had the goods, when you noticed the fault, it's seriousness and how reasonable it is for a problem of this kind to develop in such a short period of time.

"You'll have to take it up with the manufacturer"

Wrong. You bought the goods from the shop. Your contract was with them, not the company which made the item. If the goods genuinely don't work, the shop has not kept its side of the contract and you have a right to your money back. The shop will have its own claim against the supplier.

"We'll give you a credit note"

No. If the goods are faulty, you're entitled to your money back. You don't have to accept a credit note.

"Sorry, it's out of guarantee"

This can be tricky. The failure of an expensive video recorder three months out of guarantee

can mean a large repair bill. Raise it with the dealer and ask to talk to the manager. Produce the documentation and use the manufacturer's literature (which probably stresses reliability and quality) to point out that it is not reasonable to expect a failure after such a short period. There's no hard and fast law about what is reasonable in terms of a product failure. It depends on the circumstances and on the customer's ability to make their case.

"We don't give refunds on sale goods"

Wrong. Unless the fault was pointed out to you, or was something you should have seen before you bought them, goods bought in sales carry the full protection of the *Sale of Goods Act 1979.*

"We'll give you a replacement"

Only if that's what you want. However, if by now the fault has made you decide that you don't really want the product after all, you are entitled to your money back - not a replacement; and it's up to **you** to choose what to do.

SORTING THINGS OUT

If you are not satisfied with something you have paid for...

• **Stop using it immediately and take it back**, with the receipt, to the shop where you bought it. Your contract was with the shop, not the manufacturer, so it is the shop which has responsibility for dealing with your complaint.

• **Try to be as clear as you can about the problem.** If it seems appropriate, it may help to state the part of the law on which you are basing your claim. A faulty stop button on a personal stereo indicates that the equipment is not of *satisfactory quality*.

• **Decide what you want the shop to do.** Do you want your money back, or would you be happy to exchange the item for one that works?

• **If the shop assistant seems unable or unwilling to help, ask to see the manager.**

• **If you remain dissatisfied**, further options include writing to the company head office or seeking advice from the Citizens Advice Bureau or local consumer advice centre. In some cases, the CAB can ring up the trader on your behalf. If the goods were bought with a credit card you may also be able to take up your claim with the credit card company, (see page 123).

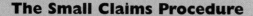

The Small Claims Procedure

If you cannot deal satisfactorily with a problem of faulty goods or poor service, you can write to the person concerned warning that you will try to recover the money they owe by taking your case to the court using the small claims procedure. This is an informal way of settling disputes, at relatively low cost, in which a judge hears your case in private, without the expense of lawyers. Claims for £3000 or less can be made under this procedure. The Lord Chancellor has announced his intention of increasing the small claims limit to £5000 in April 1999. Further details are available from your local county court, Citizens Advice Bureau or consumer advice centre.

GOODS AND SERVICES

Discrimination

It is against the law to discriminate against a customer on grounds of sex, ethnic group or disability.

The Disability Discrimination Act 1995 makes it unlawful to refuse to serve someone or to treat them less favourably because of their disability - unless this treatment can be reasonably justified. A hairdresser who refuses to give an appointment to a man or woman with a facial disfigurement is breaking the law, as are the staff in a cafe who deliberately delay serving disabled customers.

The Act applies to organisations serving or supplying goods and services directly to the public (whether for free or in return for payment), but does not require shops to stock special products for disabled customers.

Someone feeling they have been discriminated against unfairly on grounds of disability should seek advice straightaway. Help is available on the Disability Discrimination Information Line, see **Contacts** for details.

Have you got the right money?

If you have no change and offer to pay with a £10 note the shopkeeper doesn't have to sell you the goods. Strictly speaking, a trader does not have to serve a client who cannot give the exact amount of money. Nor are traders in England and Wales obliged to accept payment in notes issued by banks in Scotland or Northern Ireland nor coins issued by the Channel Islands or the Isle of Man.

Post offices and banks will accept damaged notes - as long as they meet the following conditions. There must be more than half the note remaining, it must not be in more than four pieces, the serial number must be visible, as must be at least one third of the chief cashier's signature and the sentence "I promise to pay the bearer". If the note is so badly damaged that it is not accepted, it may be worth sending it to the Bank of England with an explanation of the circumstances. Special forms for this are available from banks and post offices.

CREDIT

Buying goods on credit is usually more expensive than paying by cash because of the interest charged on the loan. This is given as the APR, the *Annual Percentage Rate*, and shows the full rate of interest to be paid. Generally, the lower the APR, the better the deal.

Before giving credit, the lender may want to establish the customer's credit worthiness. The company will check the customer's record with probably one of two credit reference agencies, who have information on almost every adult in Britain. You have a legal right, for a small charge, to see a copy of your file which is held by an agency. If you have been refused credit, and want to know which agency the lender used, you must write to the lender within 28 days of being turned down. If the information they hold on you is incorrect, you can ask for your file to be changed. For more information contact the Citizens Advice Bureau, a consumer advice centre or the Office of Fair Trading, see **Contacts**.

Store cards

These allow customers to buy goods up to a certain value, at one particular store or group of shops. The bill is either paid off in full or in fixed monthly payments. Interest is usually charged on the amount left unpaid.

GOODS AND SERVICES

Credit cards

Visa, MasterCard and other credit cards can be used in many shops and garages and also abroad. Cardholders have a limit up to which they can spend, but *they* decide how much to pay off, as long as it is above a certain minimum. This is usually £5 or a percentage of the total debt, whichever is greater. Interest is not charged if the balance is paid in full at the end of each month.

If you are not satisfied with something you bought by credit card and the shop refuses to give you a refund, you can claim your money back from the credit card company instead. Under the *Consumer Credit Act 1974* the credit card company shares responsibility with the shop for problems with any purchase that you have bought with the credit card costing more than £100. (Some credit card companies have lowered this figure to £50.) A credit card company can be easier to persuade than a reluctant shop - and you don't need to have paid all or even most of the price of the item by credit card, as long as the total price is over the set limit of £50 or £100.

Hire Purchase and Credit Sales Agreements

These are used typically for the purchase of expensive items, such as cars or furniture.

All the sums are worked out when the goods are bought and the customer is told exactly how much he or she will have to pay, over what period and what the overall cost will be. All this information must be provided, by law, as a protection against unexpected interest charges.

If you buy something on HP, the shop sells it not to you, but to a finance company. You then hire it back from the finance company for a fixed period of time, at the end of which the company sells it to you for a small sum (hence hire purchase). Only then, technically, is it yours to do with what you like.

Under a credit sales agreement, the goods belong to you straight away and so you can sell them to someone else whenever you like. But if there is still money owing, you will still have to pay off the rest of your debt.

CREDIT

Second thoughts

What do you do if you sign a credit deal and then change your mind? If you signed the credit agreement at *home*, you will receive through the post a second copy of that agreement from the finance company. You have *five days* from the time this arrives to cancel the agreement. An agreement for credit arranged in the *shop* or other *business premises* is harder to break, unless the form has to be sent away to the finance company for signature. In this case, the contract or agreement will not have been completed, and you will have a **short period** in which to stop the agreement, if you act quickly.

Never sign an agreement without all the details being filled in and try, if you can, to get a written quotation to take home to study before you agree to anything.

If the goods are faulty

Don't stop your payments until you've exhausted all possibilities.

TRY TO WIN THE SUNSHINE BACK INTO HIS CLOUDED HEART.

If you just can't get anywhere then stop the payments and, at the same time, write to the finance company explaining what you are doing and why. With luck they will put pressure on the supplier to put matters right.

If you paid for the goods by credit card you may be able to claim your money back from the credit card company instead. For further information see the section on **Credit cards**, above.

If you can't keep up the payments

Contact the lender at once and explain what has happened. You may be able to make smaller monthly payments by extending the period of the loan until you are in a better financial position. You may also want to contact a debt advisory service, such as the Citizens Advice Bureau.

If you have bought the goods on **HP** and payment is overdue, the finance company must give at least seven days notice before taking action against you. If you have already paid a third or more of the purchase price, the finance company must first obtain a court order before demanding back the goods.

LEISURE

GOING OUT

STAYING IN

THE OPEN AIR

HOLIDAYS

PUBS

The licensing laws controlling the sale of drinks were introduced in the First World War, and it's only in the last few years that they have begun to change.

Provided they sell soft drinks and food, pubs can now apply for a children's certificate, which allows children under 14 into a bar, as long as they are accompanied by an adult. However the children must leave the bar by 9pm.

A 14 year old is allowed into the bar of a pub, but only for soft drinks and at the licensee's discretion. At 16 and 17 a young person can buy beer, cider or perry, but only to drink with a meal in the dining or restaurant area of a pub. Only at 18 is someone allowed to buy alcohol or drink alcohol in a bar. Drinks with 0.5% or less of alcohol, such as some canned shandy and low alcohol beers, are not regarded as intoxicating liquor for licensing purposes.

It is an offence to sell alcohol to anyone under 18 - unless it can be shown that the landlord or landlady did their best to check that the person was 18 or over. It's also an offence to try to buy alcohol for someone under 18. The maximum fine for this is £1,000, and licensees stand to lose their license after more than one conviction.

Licensees have the right to ban or refuse to serve anyone they choose - as long as it is not because of the person's sex, colour, ethnic group or disability. They have the *duty* not to serve someone who looks as if they've had enough to drink already.

Licensees can be charged with "permitting drunkenness" and fined. All measures of alcohol are legally controlled. Until recently the froth on the top of a glass of beer formed part of the pint. However, if the *Weights and Measures (Beer and Cider) Bill*, currently in front of Parliament, becomes law, beer drinkers can expect to receive a full pint, with the measure clearly marked on the side of the glass.

GOING OUT

EATING OUT
Quality

Whether you're in an expensive restaurant or an ordinary café you have the same right to reject any food of a quality below the standard that you are reasonably entitled to expect. What is 'reasonable' depends on such things as the price charged, what the menu says, and basic standards. The laws applying to faulty goods or services also apply here. (See pages 114-120).

It's advisable to complain as soon as you think there's a problem. The more you are paying, the higher the standard you're entitled to expect.

If the quality of your meal is poor or the service is bad, you are entitled to make a reasonable deduction from the bill, but don't leave without paying. Explain to the manager why you are not satisfied, and leave your name and address. The restaurant can take this up with you later if it wishes.

Booking

If you book a table but don't arrive, the restaurant is entitled to make a charge if it has not been able to fill the table. If, on the other hand, you book a table which has not been kept, you can ask for compensation for the cost of the wasted journey.

Safety

Under the *Food Act 1990*, it is a criminal offence for a restaurant to serve food which is unfit for human consumption. If you are concerned about the hygiene in a restaurant or café, you can contact your local council's environmental health department or trading standards office.

These have the power to investigate, prosecute and even close premises where hygiene laws are being broken.

Prices

All restaurants, pubs and cafés must, by law, clearly display the price of food and drink where it is served.

Service charge

Sometimes a service charge, usually 10%, is added to the bill in a restaurant. If this has been indicated before you order, then you've got to pay it, unless the service was very bad. In that case, its reasonable to ask the manager for a discount. If there is no service charge, it's up to you whether to leave a tip.

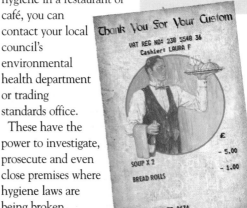

Thank You For Your Custom

VAT REG NO: 238 5548 36
Cashier: LAURA F

£

SOUP X 2   - 5.00
BREAD ROLLS   - 1.00

6610 006 32 0634

GAMBLING
Raffles

Anyone can organise a raffle, as long as the proceeds are for a society, club or charity and not for profit or private gain - but it may need to be registered with the local authority. The Citizens Advice Bureau can give you guidance on the legal requirements.

Bingo

Players must be at least 18 years old. There may be charges for admission and participation which the club is obliged to display, by law. Winnings in commercial clubs are subject to a minimum tax of 10%.

Bets

Bets cannot be enforced by law. If the loser fails to pay, he or she cannot be taken to court. This includes the bookmaker.

THE NATIONAL LOTTERY

8

Lottery tickets or scratch cards may only be sold to someone aged 16 or over. Retailers who sell tickets or scratch cards to people under 16 face a fine or even imprisonment. The deadline for ticket sales is 7.30pm on the night of the draw. Players have up to two hours after the purchase of a ticket to check that the numbers on the printed slip are correct.

Prizes can be claimed up to 180 days after the draw. All retail outlets can pay out prizes of up to £75 and selected outlets up to £500. Prizes up to £10,000 can be claimed from post offices. Claims for all other prizes should be made through a National Lottery Regional Centre. For further information contact the National Lottery, tel 0645 100 000.

32

If you are one of a group of people who jointly buy lottery tickets each week it's a good idea to draw up an agreement in advance about how any winnings will be shared. The winnings of a husband or wife who buy a ticket from joint funds belong to both partners.

29

14

THEATRE, CINEMA, SPORT

If you go to a show and spend the evening looking at nothing more than a concrete pillar it may be worth complaining and asking for a refund. It's no excuse for the management to say that you should have arrived earlier or booked a better seat. Under the law of contract they should have warned you the view was restricted before selling you the ticket.

There is no simple law setting out people's rights in the event of a change to the advertised programme or the cancellation of a performance. The position will depend on such things as advanced publicity, information given when the ticket was sold and the circumstances which forced a change of plan.

Although disgruntled spectators have been successful in taking promoters to court, legal action is not recommended for disappointment over a cancelled event. Some promoters will try to retain public goodwill by offering tickets for another performance, or refunds. If they don't, it's worth explaining why you think their action is *unreasonable* - a key word in cases of this kind.

Three Leicester City football supporters went to watch their team play a cup match at Millwall. However, they saw little of the game because their view was obscured by a pylon, a safety fence and one of the stands. They eventually sued Millwall Football Club in court, where they were awarded their travel expenses, a third off the price of their ticket, plus costs.

STAYING IN

TELEVISION
Licence

A licence is required if anyone in a household uses a television or video recorder. The current licence fee is £97.50 for a colour TV and £32.50 for a black and white set (April 1998).

A single licence covers all TV equipment in a household. If the house is divided in to *separate* flats or bedsitting rooms a licence is required for the television equipment in each room.

However, only one licence is required when a house is shared with the television placed in a communal area. Separate licences are needed for a TV or video in a second home - but not if the set is used in a touring caravan or houseboat which is not a permanent residence.

A special licence is available to people who are retired and of pensionable age, who are disabled, mentally handicapped or mentally ill and who live in a residential home or nursing home or in sheltered accommodation run by a local authority or housing association. This is known as an ARC licence (standing for accommodation for residential care). It costs £5 and can only be obtained by those responsible for the residential care or housing.

A person who is blind can obtain a reduction of £1.25 on the cost of a licence or may purchase a sound only TV, for which no licence is required.

Videotapes

Strictly speaking, you may record a TV or radio programme only to allow you to watch or listen to it at a more convenient time. Keeping films or programmes on tape for longer than this is unlawful.

THE TELEPHONE

BT publishes a free guide outlining the services and products it can offer older and disabled people - including a free extension bell for customers who are hard of hearing and the *Light User Scheme,*

Complaints

If you wish to complain about the accuracy or the presentation of issues in a particular programme you can ring or write to the relevant broadcasting company. See **Contacts** for details.

STAYING IN

providing a rebate for those customers whose quarterly charges are below a certain level. Dial Freephone 150 for further information.

There is no national scheme providing financial help with the cost of telephones for older people - but help may be available to someone who is chronically sick or disabled. Under the *Chronically Sick and Disabled Persons Act 1970*, local authorities have a duty to help people who have certain disabilities with the costs of obtaining a telephone. The kind of person likely to qualify will have severely restricted mobility, live alone and be at some risk without access to a phone. In such cases it is the local authority which decides whether there is such a need.

If you receive Income Support you may be able to get a budgeting loan (which must be repaid) to meet some telephone costs. See **Contacts** for other organisations offering advice and information.

ENTERTAINING

You invite some friends around for the evening and one of them falls down the stairs. If the cause of the accident was the state of the carpet, you could be liable for their injuries. This doesn't mean wrapping every sharp corner in cotton wool, but something like a loose piece of stair carpet definitely should be fixed, since it is reasonable for visitors to expect to walk down the stairs safely. You're not expected to guard against the *unforeseeable*. If someone has too much to drink, tumbles down stairs and breaks a leg, that's their fault, not yours.

I'M THE INSURANCE MAN, MADAM---
I CALLED TO SEE IF YOU
ARE FULLY COVERED!

Insurance

If someone is injured in your home they may be able to get compensation through your insurance policy. Most householders' insurance policies cover owners for injuries to other people (called "third parties") caused by the state of the buildings or its fittings. If you're in rented accommodation, your landlord could be liable - and again it is his or her insurance company that would pay damages. If you face this problem, it's worth checking with a solicitor.

CITIZENSHIP
FOUNDATION

STAYING IN

PETS

Under the *Protection of Animals Act 1911*, owners have a legal responsibility to care for their animals and to make sure they do not suffer unnecessarily. It is an offence to be cruel to the animal, or to abandon it, if it is likely to cause the animal unnecessary suffering.

Pet owners are also responsible for any damage their animal causes if they knew (or should have known) it was likely to cause such damage, or if their animal is defined as *dangerous*. (In law, dangerous animals are those which are not domesticated in this country and might be expected to have dangerous characteristics, eg a monkey or snake.) Most household insurance policies cover the holder against damage to a third party by their pet.

Under the *Control of Dogs Order 1992*, anyone owning a dog must make sure it wears a collar, with the name and address of its owner, when it is in a public place. Most areas have local by-laws making it an offence to allow a dog to foul the footpath.

Lisa had to go away unexpectedly. After she had been gone for six days, one of her neighbours called the RSPCA and told them that she thought Lisa's pet rat, Ziggy, was in need of care. They found the animal with just a scrap of cheese and no water. It was dehydrated, trembling and close to death. When she returned, Lisa said that she had asked someone to feed and water the rat - but they had let her down. She was charged and found guilty of causing the animal unnecessary suffering. Lisa, who was unemployed, was fined £80 and told to pay £50 towards the cost of the case.

It is also an offence under the *Dangerous Dogs Act 1991*, to allow a dog to be dangerously out of control in a public place. The owner, or person in charge of a dog which injures someone can be fined or imprisoned for up to six months. The court can also have the dog destroyed and disqualify the owner from keeping a dog in the future. A farmer is allowed to shoot a dog that is not under anyone's control and is worrying livestock on her or his land.

Under the *Guard Dog Act 1975*, guard dogs should be under the control of a handler or else tied up and not be able to roam freely. A warning notice should also be displayed. The Act does not apply to private houses or farm land.

Difficulty in caring for a pet

When someone goes into hospital or is placed by the local authority in residential care or a nursing home, the local authority has a duty under the *National Assistance Act 1948* to make sure that the householder's property is properly protected - and this includes the care of their pets. If the person is unable to find suitable care for their animal, the local authority will find an appropriate temporary home. It may ask for a contribution to the cost from the owner.

The Cinnamon Trust operates a pet fostering service for pets whose owners have gone into hospital or have moved to accommodation where pets are not accepted. See **Contacts** for further details.

You can specify in your will how you would like your animal to be cared for after your death - eg, by a friend or charitable organisation - as long as their agreement has been obtained beforehand. For more information on wills, see page 34.

CITIZENSHIP
FOUNDATION

THE OPEN AIR

WALKING

Stepping on to a piece of land marked *"trespassers will be prosecuted"* will not propel you straight into court. Trespass is not a crime - it's a civil offence. A landowner can require the trespasser to leave, but in doing so may use only a reasonable amount of force. If the trespasser refuses to go, the landowner should call the police.

National Grid ... 182
ORDNANCE SURVEY
New Popular Edition
ONE-INCH MAP
of ENGLAND & WALES
BRIGHTON &
WORTHING
Sheet 182

First Published 1940
Full Revision 1933 Reach 1946 with later corrections

Price (Paper) Four Shillings & Sixpence Net

Footpaths

If a route across a piece of land has been used for 20 years or more without interruption, that route becomes a right of way. A footpath cannot be lost by disuse. Once a right of way has been established it can be used by the public forever or until it is closed by an order made under the *Highways Act 1980* or the *Town and Country Planning Act 1990*.

Strictly speaking, footpaths are for walkers only. It's a criminal offence to ride a cycle or motor bike or drive a car on a path. Footpaths are shown on Ordnance Survey maps - but if you need to check a path, you can look at the maps in the local council planning office. Under the *Rights of Way Act 1990*, a landowner who ploughs or plants any crop (except grass) over a public footpath must, within 14 days, make sure that the line of the path is clear to anyone using it. It is also an offence to put up a misleading sign, such as "private" which discourages people from using a public right of way. If you come across a problem of this kind and want something done, contact the landowner, or the local council.

The local council's Rights of Way Officer has a duty to make sure that public rights of way are kept open and free from obstruction. It's the local authority's responsibility to maintain footpaths so that people can walk along them, and the job of the landowner to look after stiles and gates along the path.

Beaches

Land between the low and high tide line is the property of the Crown - and there is almost never any problem in walking along a beach. But there is no right to get onto a beach over private land, unless there is a public right of way.

THE OPEN AIR

Bulls

Checking your legal rights here means being able to tell one breed of bull from another without getting too close. Since 1981, all dairy bulls (such Friesan, Guernsey and Jersey) are banned from fields crossed by public paths - and other types of bull are allowed only if they are in with cows or heifers - which make them much less aggressive.

Wildlife

Under the *Wild Mammals Protection Act 1996*, it is unlawful to inflict intentionally any unnecessary suffering on a wild mammal. Anyone found guilty is liable to a fine and/or up to six months imprisonment. The *Wildlife and Countryside Act 1981* gives protection to a wide range of wild animals, birds and plants, and covers killing, injuring, taking or possessing and disturbing the place of shelter or protection. For an up-to-date list of all protected species, see Whitakers Almanack, available in most libraries.

BOATING

There is a public right to use a canoe or boat only on the *tidal* section of a river. Above this point, permission to use the river is needed from the owner of the river bank.

A licence is also needed to use a boat or canoe on a canal - obtainable from British Waterways (the number of the local office is in the 'phone book), and the British Canoe Union.

"GEOGRAPHIA"
Ramblers' Map
JERSEY
(Scale 2 inches to 1 mile)

PRICE 1/-

Published by
"GEOGRAPHIA" LTD
167 Fleet Street, London, E.C.4.

THE OPEN AIR

FISHING

You can fish at any time in the sea and in tidal waters, unless there are local by-laws forbidding it. Fishing off a pier usually needs a licence. Anyone, aged 12 or over, fishing for salmon, trout, freshwater fish or eels must have an Environment Agency Rod Fishing Licence, available from post offices. The licence allows the holder to fish anywhere in England and Wales, but permission is still required from the landowner or the person owning the fishing rights.

Pollution

The Environment Agency asks members of the public to report any environmental incident - on rivers, lakes, canals or the coastline - by ringing their local Environment Agency office (in the 'phone book), or by using the free 24 hour number, 0800 80 70 60.

ALLOTMENTS

Under the *Smallholdings and Allotments Act 1908*, district councils and outer London boroughs have a duty to provide enough allotments where they believe there is demand for them. *The London Government Act 1963* gives inner London boroughs the discretion whether to provide allotments if they feel there is sufficient demand. If allotments are taken over and used for other purposes, the council has a duty to provide tenants with an equivalent amount of land for allotment purposes, unless such provision is unnecessary.

HOTELS

Proprietors of inns and hotels in the UK have a legal duty to provide food and accommodation to anyone who asks - as long as not all rooms have been let and the person is in a fit state and able and

Dorothy noticed that the water in Ackhurst Brook near Wigan, where she lived, was an unusual colour - particularly around the discharge pipe used by a local factory. She rang the Environment Agency, who sent an officer to investigate. The officer reported that the water was discoloured, smelt foul and contained pieces of food which looked like shells from baked beans - which is just what they were. The company admitted polluting the river, contrary to the *Water Resources Act 1991* and was fined £5,000 by local magistrates.

HOLIDAYS

willing to pay. (This does not apply to bed and breakfast, boarding houses or residential hotels.)

It is a criminal offence to leave a hotel room without paying, or without the intention of paying. In these circumstances, a proprietor can hold on to (and eventually sell) any luggage that has been left until the bill has been paid - but this doesn't include a vehicle, the things left inside it, or live animals.

If anything is stolen from a guest's room, he or she can claim compensation - but the liability of the hotel or innkeeper is limited to £50 for one article or £100 in total - as long as a copy of the *Hotel Proprietors Act 1956* is exhibited where it can be conveniently read by guests. The limits do not apply if the loss was due to the negligence of the hotel.

PACKAGE HOLIDAYS

When you buy a holiday of this kind, you make a contract with the travel organiser - that is, the company responsible for arranging the package. This is usually the tour operator, but can also be the travel agent, particularly if you have asked for elements to be added to the holiday, not included in the brochure.

Although holiday brochures are designed to show a hotel or resort at its best, the *Package Travel, Package Holidays and Package Tours Regulations 1992* state they must be accurate and not misleading. If the facilities you are promised, such as a swimming pool or a room with a view, do not materialise, then you may be able to obtain compensation because of the failure of the company organising the holiday to keep its side of the contract. Under the *Trade Descriptions Act 1968* it is an offence for a firm to make a misleading statement about the goods or services it provides, which it knows to be false - but this is something which is usually taken up by local trading standards officers.

Before you sign or hand over any money, it's important to read the small print and to check what it says about amendments or alterations to your schedule. Travel organisers can, in certain circumstances, make changes to accommodation, flight times etc., *provided they make this clear in the brochure or contract.*

Travel organisers must provide general information about passport and visa requirements, health formalities, surcharges and additional taxes. They should also explain their arrangements for repaying money and getting travellers home if the company fails. Again, this is all explained in the *Package Travel Regulations*, mentioned above.

It is important to inform the travel agent or airline *at the time of booking* of any special needs - such as physical disability or medical and dietary requirements. You are entitled to take medicines abroad - as long as they are for your own use during your stay. It's a good idea to leave the medicines in their original packaging and keep a copy of your prescription.

If you pay all or part of the cost of the holiday by credit card, you may be able to claim a full or partial refund from the *credit card company* if the company organising the travel fails to keep its side of the contract. This may be easier than trying to obtain redress through the tour operator. For more information on paying by credit card, see page 123.

Delays

In selling you the ticket, the airline agrees to fly you between two airports, but there is no strict legal obligation to fly you at the times, or even on the day, printed on the ticket. Although some airlines and travel companies do offer passengers food and accommodation if there is a major delay, it is not something they have to do by law.

However, there are set rates of compensation for passengers who have booked a ticket, but fail to get a seat on a plane that has been *overbooked*. If there are no seats available on a flight from an airport in the UK or European Union and you have booked on a scheduled service and arrived at the airport in good time - you are entitled to cash compensation there and then. The airline may offer you travel vouchers, but you can insist on cash.

Medical costs and insurance

If you are travelling in the European Union, complete Form E111 (available from post offices) allowing you free or reduced medical costs, and take the form with you on holiday.

A good travel insurance policy will compensate you for losses while you're away and even illness before you go. Don't forget to take the policy with you on holiday so that, if anything goes wrong, you can make sure you keep to the terms of the agreement.

HOLIDAYS

If your holiday includes a dangerous activity, like skiing, or you are going to a country where you would have to pay for your own medical treatment, it's worth buying medical insurance before you go - but check that it covers the sort of thing you are planning to do. If you are ill or hurt you may have to pay for treatment yourself and then claim the money back when you get home. It is important to keep receipts and other documents as evidence for your claim.

To know more about travel requirements or conditions, you can ring the embassy of the country concerned, or contact the Foreign and Commonwealth Office, tel 0171 238 4503 for advice about security conditions.

Passports

A passport is usually valid for 10 years and can be used for travel to any country in the world. However, some countries require visitors' passports to be valid for a period of time *beyond* the duration of their stay - and this can be as much as a year. Therefore if your passport is in, or nearing, its final year of validity, you may need to apply for another. Your travel agent should be able to advise you.

COMING HOME

The amount of goods - and particularly alcohol - that you can bring back into Britain depends on the country from which you are returning. The allowances are more generous when returning to Britain from a country inside the EU (but are likely to cease entirely at the end of June 1999).

Customs officials can check your baggage for prohibited goods (such as drugs, weapons, obscene materials and threats to public health) or to see if you need to pay tax or duty if you are coming from or have travelled through a country outside the European Union. For more details of the powers and duties of customs officers contact your local Customs and Excise office (under "C" in the 'phone book) for a copy of the *Traveller's Charter*. Also available is *Complaints and putting things right*, the Customs and Excise code of practice.

HOLIDAYS

TAKING A CAR OR MOTORCYCLE

You'll normally need to get a *Green Card* from your insurance company, which extends your insurance cover to countries other than Great Britain.

If you're driving to Spain, it is advisable to take out a Bail Bond (*fianza*) as well. Under Spanish law the car and driver can be detained after an accident, but can be released on production of a Bail Bond. The Bond will also help cover the cost of any legal action or fine. Contact your insurance company for both the Green Card and Bail Bond.

If you are in an accident, tell the police and ask for a record or receipt - it will help you with your insurance claim when you get home. It's a good idea to take notes and photographs of the accident - including pictures of the number plates of the vehicles involved.

Don't sign anything in a language that you don't understand. If you're put under pressure, write *"I don't understand"* immediately above your signature.

HELP WITH ORGANISATION AND FINANCE

A number of organisations, including Saga, provide for older people geared to a wide range of interests and needs. Local travel agents have details. Age Concern groups and social services also arrange special holidays - for details contact your local group, Citizens Advice Bureau or social services, who can also advise on the availability of small grants to help with the cost. Help is also available through the *National Benevolent Fund for the Aged* for people in receipt of Income Support, Housing Benefit or Council Tax Benefit and who have been recently ill or bereaved or who have not had a holiday for at least five years. See **Contacts** for details.

HOLIDAYS

PENSION AND OTHER BENEFITS

While you are away on holiday in Britain, you can cash up to two pension or benefit payments at any post office. If you are likely to be away for longer than this you can collect a form from a post office signifying a temporary change of address and arrange to collect the payments from a post office where you are staying.

If you go overseas and draw a weekly state pension, it can be left to build up for up to three months for collection when you return. Your local Benefits Agency office will be able to tell you what to do if you are going away for longer than this.

IF SOMETHING GOES WRONG
Holiday Disappointment

If you have a problem with your holiday organised by a tour operator or travel agent, tell the company, or their representative, as soon as possible. If the matter is not dealt with, make a detailed note and contact the travel firm as soon as you get home.

If you're still not satisfied with their response, get in touch with the Citizens Advice Bureau. They can advise you on what to do next and, if you choose, how to take your claim to the small claims court (see page 120). If the travel organiser belongs to ABTA, contact them also. If they are unable to help directly, ABTA can arrange for independent arbitration, see **Contacts**.

Lost and stolen

If your luggage doesn't arrive, report the loss immediately. Try to get a copy of any reports you complete. Under international law, the airline is responsible for lost or damaged luggage, but compensation is paid by weight, rather than value. Therefore it may be better to claim through your holiday or household insurance.

If you run out of money, even overseas, you can go to a bank and arrange for money to be transferred from your own bank or building society at home. There will probably be a charge, but it should arrive within 24 hours.

HOLIDAYS

If you lose anything valuable tell the police and get a note from them confirming that you have done this. Contact the travel company if you lose your ticket home and immediately report the loss of the traveller's cheques or credit cards to the bank or credit company. They often let you reverse the charges for the call. It is very important to report losses to your insurance company within the time limit given in the policy.

If your passport is lost or stolen overseas, inform the local police and contact the nearest British Consulate which should be able to provide help or advice. The police should also be informed if it happens in Britain.

In trouble

Travellers overseas are automatically subject to the laws of the country they are visiting. If you're arrested, insist on the British Consulate being informed. The Consulate will explain the local procedures, including availability of legal aid and access to lawyers.

Illness and death

Health care for British people overseas falls into one of three categories: countries in the European Union, countries outside this with which the UK has a reciprocal health care agreement, and countries with *no* health agreement with the UK. Most countries fit into the last category. If you are taken ill in a country with which there is a reciprocal health care agreement, you normally receive free emergency treatment, but you may have to pay for prescribed medicines. However the cost of this can sometimes be claimed back on your return. Useful information is given in *Health Advice for Travellers*, leaflet T6, produced by the Department of Health and available from post offices, libraries and the Citizens Advice Bureau. Leaflet T6 includes form E111, which can be used to obtain emergency treatment in the European Union.

SAFETY

CRIME

VICTIM SUPPORT

COMPENSATION

KEEPING SAFE

CRIME

Our fear of crime is often greater than it need be. The actual percentage of people who become victims of violent crime is very small, and it is young men - rather than women or older people - who have the greatest chance of something happening to them. Surveys have shown that the older the head of the household, the less likely the household is to be burgled.

This chapter has been written to explain, in general terms, the law surrounding certain crimes and to indicate some of the choices open to people who are unlucky enough to become a victim, or who wish to take measures to protect themselves against such a thing happening.

THEFT

There are, in law, three parts to theft. A person is guilty of theft if they (i) dishonestly take something, which (ii) belongs to someone else, and (iii) intend to deprive that person of it permanently.

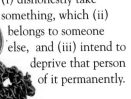

Robbery

Stealing something with the use or threat of force.

Burglary

Burglary takes place when a person enters a building, or part of a building, without permission, intending to steal, cause unlawful damage, seriously harm or rape someone. Even if nothing is taken or done, a crime has still been committed. It's enough in law to prove that the person intended to break the law in this way.

ASSAULT AND BATTERY

The word assault is not used in law in quite the same way as in everyday speech. Strictly speaking, an assault takes place when a person causes someone to fear that they are about to suffer unlawful physical violence.

Battery describes the act of hitting a person or intentionally using force on someone without their consent.

Normally assault and battery take place at the same time. However, it is possible to be assaulted without battery (raising an arm and shouting threats without striking anyone) and

CRIME

battered without assault (hitting someone from behind without warning).

Actual bodily harm (ABH), malicious wounding and grievous bodily harm

ABH means that the victim has suffered injury such as bruising or shock. More serious are the offences of malicious wounding and grievous bodily harm. Wounding requires breaking of the skin and grievous bodily harm refers to serious injury or harm.

ACTING IN SELF DEFENCE

When someone is faced with an attacker, the law says that he or she may use *reasonable* force in self-defence. This means that they can fight back and defend themselves but should not go too far and seriously injure their attacker, otherwise they also commit an offence. It is also acceptable to use reasonable force in order to prevent a crime, to assist in the lawful arrest of an offender and in the defence of property.

Victim Charged With Assault!

Alan bought an old car for £200, which he intended to restore. He parked it on a piece of waste land close to his home. A few days later he received a 'phone call telling him that some youngsters were wrecking the vehicle. Alan ran to where the car was parked to find three boys jumping on the roof and every light and mirror had been smashed.

"I managed to grab two of them but the third got away," he said later. "In my anger I slapped each one across the face and told them to get their fathers. One was left with a hand print on his face and the other had a cut lip, but I suspect that was caused in a fall and had nothing to do with me."

Shortly after the incident, Alan was questioned by police and charged with assault. In court he pleaded guilty and was ordered to pay the boys, aged 10 and 11, £25 each plus £54 costs. No action was taken against the boys who, Alan said, had caused about £400 damage to his car.

CRIME

CITIZEN'S ARREST

Anyone who sees a person committing a serious offence or has reasonable grounds for believing that they have committed one, can make a *citizen's arrest*. But it is important to take care! Men and women have been hurt and even killed trying to do their civic duty. The best advice is to take in as much as you can about the incident, and then ring the police. But if you do get involved, remember that a member of the public only has the power to make an arrest for a *serious* offence, such as theft, serious assault, or burglary. Don't arrest someone parking on a double yellow line - unless you want to end up in court yourself.

Neighbourhood patrols come up against the same problem. They can't arrest someone who they think is *about* to commit an offence (it must already have been done). Nor can they use excessive force - otherwise they may face charges of assault and wrongful arrest.

HARASSMENT

Under the *Public Order Act 1986*, it is an offence to use threatening, abusive or insulting words or behaviour in public in a way that is intended to cause a person harassment, alarm or distress. It is also an offence to put up a sign or poster that is threatening or abusive in the same way. The law is designed to protect anyone who is being treated like this because, for example, of their race, disability or sexuality. Harassment of this kind is a crime, just like any other, and can be reported to the police, who have a duty to investigate and to try to find those responsible. Statements from witnesses will strengthen a case.

Under the *Protection from Harassment Act 1997*, it is an offence for a person, through their behaviour, to harass someone or make them afraid that violence may be used against them. It's no defence for the person to say they didn't mean any harm. An offence is committed if it is felt that, in the circumstances, any reasonable person would feel harassed or fear violence. The Act states that the actions or course of

CRIME

conduct must take place on at least two occasions.

Anyone who is a victim of this may seek a court injunction preventing the person from behaving in this way and may also try to obtain damages for the anxiety caused and any financial loss, for example, through time off work.

Under the *Race Relations Act 1976*, councils have a duty to help if tenants or home-owners in their area are racially harassed or attacked. For further details, see page 42.

What if it happens to me?

What you actually do depends on the situation. If it's an isolated incident and the person is someone you don't know, then it may be best to try and ignore it. If you react and get abusive yourself, you run the risk of finding yourself in a far worse position.

If it's happened before, or you're being harassed where you live, then it's important for your own safety to tell the police. If you are receiving abuse at work, try and sort it out with the people concerned but, if that doesn't work, raise it with your supervisor or manager. See also page 60.

Someone suffering serious abuse or harassment may be able to claim compensation from the *Criminal Injuries Compensation Authority*, see page 150 and **Contacts**.

"In there!" he gasped. "Three of them. 'Ware the old man. He's a tiger."

Indecent assault

Under the *Sexual Offences Act 1956*, it is an offence to touch or threaten a person in an indecent way. Groping and unwanted fondling can come into this category. Indecent assault carries a punishment of up to ten years imprisonment.

Rape

A male, over the age of ten, who has either vaginal or anal intercourse with someone who doesn't want him to and who knows that this person is not consenting or takes no care as to whether she or he does, commits the crime of rape. It's also an offence under the *Sexual Offences Act 1956* to threaten or force a person to have sex against their will, or to give them drugs in the hope that they will give in.

Forcing another person to have sex is rape, and it's no defence for the man to say he was drunk. Rape also occurs when the victim is too far gone through alcohol or other drugs to know what they were doing.

A wife is not obliged to have sex with her husband. If she does not consent, it's rape. See

pages 175.

Most police stations now have women officers who have been trained to deal with victims of sexual offences in a sensitive way. A female victim can ask to be examined by a female doctor, and may be accompanied by a friend or relative.

The police will be able to gather evidence more easily if the rape or assault is reported as soon as possible. Reporting the crime early also makes the evidence more believable in court.

Once a person explains to the police that they have been sexually assaulted or raped, or someone has been charged with these offences, the victim has a right, in law, to remain

anonymous. Neither their name and address nor their picture can appear in the press or media.

Help is also available from *Victim Support*, a *Rape Crisis Centre* (who will talk to any girl or woman who has suffered an unpleasant sexual experience) or *Survivors* (offering an advice service for men). See **Contacts** for details. Victims of rape can apply for compensation to the *Criminal Injuries Compensation Authority*. See page 150 and **Contacts**.

Male victims of rape are treated in law in the same way as female victims.

If you are accused of rape, contact a solicitor immediately. Rape is a serious crime, and the punishment can be severe.

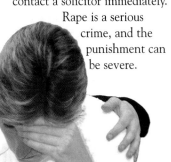

ABUSIVE TELEPHONE CALLS

It is an offence under the *Telecommunications Act 1984* to make threatening 'phone calls. Heavy breathing, rude words and intimate questions are all against the law, and carry a sentence of up to six months in prison and a fine of up to £5,000.

If you get such a call, try not to react. Don't start talking to the caller and don't blow a whistle down the 'phone. Remember you're in control. Don't hang up, but put the receiver down and walk away for a few minutes. Try to do something else, and then put the handset back without checking if the caller is still there. If the 'phone rings again you can pick up the receiver and not say anything - a genuine caller will speak first. If you dial 1471, you can usually obtain the number of the 'phone from which you have just been called.

If the calls carry on, you can report it to BT and the police. It's very easy to trace calls today, and BT run a free Helpline on 0800 666700.

CITIZENSHIP
FOUNDATION

CALLING THE POLICE

There is no law stating that anyone who sees a crime must inform the police. But if those responsible are to be dealt with by the courts, calling the police is the only way of doing this. Victims of violent crime may be entitled to compensation for their injuries (see below), but before this can be claimed, the crime must be reported to the police.

If you are a victim of a crime and report the incident to the police, you will be given a crime number and the name of the officer dealing with the case. The police should also keep you informed of any significant developments in their investigation and whether someone has been caught, cautioned or charged. They will also ask if you wish to receive further

information about the progress of your case and whether you would like to be told of the date of the trial and its outcome. This is explained in more detail in the *Victim's Charter*, see **Contacts**.

The police will also put you in touch, if you wish, with the local *Victim Support Scheme*.

If you are a victim of a serious crime which has resulted in an offender being sent to prison, you will be contacted by a probation officer, within two months of the sentence, asking whether you want to be told when the prisoner may be released. You will be asked whether you have any worries about this, and these can be taken into account when the authorities consider the conditions that may be attached to the prisoner's release. There is also a helpline, charged at local rates, which can be used if you receive any unwelcome contact from a prisoner or have concerns about their release, tel 0345 585 112.

COMPENSATION
Criminal Injuries Compensation Scheme

A state-funded scheme, providing compensation to people who suffer injury through crimes of violence.

Compensation is awarded according to the type and extent of

SAFETY

VICTIM SUPPORT

Victim Support is an independent charity offering help to victims of crime. It runs a network of local schemes using trained volunteers, and a national helpline, see **Contacts** for details.

The police normally inform Victim Support of cases of burglary, robbery, assault, arson, harassment or criminal damage to a person's home.

Within a few days, someone from the local Victim Support scheme makes contact with the victim by letter or 'phone offering to visit. The staff and volunteers are specially trained to help victims of crime cope with their experience and to give practical support with claims for insurance or compensation.

However, Victim Support is not automatically informed of cases involving rape, domestic violence, road death and bereavement through murder or manslaughter. In these situations the police will only pass on names with the agreement of those involved.

If you are a victim of crime and called to court as a witness, you can ask to see a courtroom before the case starts, have a seat reserved in court for someone accompanying you and ask to wait separately from other people involved in the case. This may be difficult in some courts, but the court staff will make arrangements wherever possible. Details of this and other help available are given in the *Victim's Charter* and the *Charter for Court Users*, see **Contacts**.

a person's injuries. The minimum award is £1,000 and does not depend on the culprit having been caught and convicted.

The scheme covers physical and mental injury, but is open only to victims who have been injured in a crime of *violence*, in an attempt to prevent an offence or detain an offender, or as a result of someone trespassing on the railway. A person injured in a normal road accident would not qualify for an award (unless they were a victim of a deliberate attempt to injure them). Nor would someone who became depressed or needed medical treatment because their house had been burgled.

Applicants must have reported the offence to the police. Delay, or failure to do so, without good reason greatly reduces the strength of their claim.

Application to the *Criminal Injuries Compensation Authority* should also be made as soon as possible. Normally claims cannot be considered more than two years after the incident that caused the injury. Details of the scheme are available from police stations, the Citizens Advice Bureau, solicitors and the Authority's head office in Glasgow. See **Contacts** for details.

Court awards

When a person is found guilty of a criminal offence, causing personal injury, loss or damage, the court can make a *compensation order*. This requires the offender to pay the victim compensation for any loss, damage or injury that they have suffered. Compensation is limited to what the offender can afford and so may not cover the full cost of the loss or injury suffered. If the offender cannot afford to pay both a fine and compensation, the court should give

priority to the payment of compensation.

It is also possible, in certain circumstances, for someone suffering assault to begin *civil*, rather than criminal, proceedings against the person responsible, in order to obtain damages for the injuries or losses caused. However, before taking action of this kind, it is advisable to speak to a solicitor. It is also worth noting that some offenders will not have the means to pay compensation.

KEEPING SAFE

A number of measures can be taken to feel more secure, both at home and elsewhere.

Security

Good quality door and window locks, a door chain and spy hole are obvious things to consider. Advice on these is available from local police crime prevention officers who will call, by prior arrangement, to advise on home security. Some local authorities provide and fit secure locks for council tenants. Local Victim Support, Age Concern and Help the Aged groups may have a list of reliable locksmiths or know of help available for buying and fitting locks.

It is not a good idea to leave keys in locks, especially those set in glass panel doors. Extra lighting at the front and rear of the property is also useful.

Callers

A number of officials, such as those from the police, the fire brigade and the water, electricity and gas companies, have a right of entry to people's homes in certain circumstances. People from these organisations should always show some form of identity and authorisation, and invariably the householder is entitled to a period of notice. Only in very exceptional circumstances can officials force their way in, for example, if there is a risk of a gas explosion, the police need to make an arrest, or when tenants or squatters are being evicted by court bailiffs.

It is obviously important to check the identity and authorisation of callers before letting them in. Don't release the door chain, if you have one, until you are sure about their identity and the purpose of their visit. If you have any doubts, it is quite alright to ask the person to wait while you contact the

By courtesy of Liverpool Daily Post & Echo Plc.

organisation they claim to represent. Alternatively, you may prefer to ask them to return on another day. Again this gives you time to check that they have a genuine reason for calling.

If you think you may be the victim of a bogus caller, contact the police straightaway. Don't feel embarrassed that you have let someone in to your home.

KEEPING SAFE

Neighbourhood Watch

Many parts of the country now have Neighbourhood Watch schemes. As well as reducing recorded crime they also encourage neighbourliness and closer communities - and have been the start of much larger projects of benefit to the whole community.

If you are interested in getting involved, your local police will be able to tell you if there is a scheme in your area or help you set up one of your own.

Outside

If you go out, especially at night, it's a good idea to tell someone where you are going. If you have to walk home, try to get someone to go with you.

Try to carry only essential items with you. Don't carry large amounts of money or valuables, unless absolutely necessary.

If someone does try to grab your bag, it's not a good idea to resist, as you may be injured in the struggle.

If you carry a screech alarm, keep it ready in your hand, not at the bottom of a bag. Try to have your car and front door keys ready as you approach the car or the house so that you can gain entry straight away. If, when you reach home, you have any suspicions that things are not quite right, *do not go in*. Dial 999 from the nearest 'phone. The police will not mind being called out.

THE
LEGAL SYSTEM

POLICE

COURTS

INFORMATION & LEGAL ADVICE

POWERS AND DUTIES

Most of the information that the police receive comes from the general public and without this help, they could do very little. Many of the police's powers and duties when investigating crime are contained in the *Police and Criminal Evidence Act 1984*.

Accompanying this Act are what are known as the *Codes of Practice* - a set of guidelines which the police must follow when investigating crime and dealing with the public at a police station. Anyone questioned at a police station has a right to see and read the Codes. Copies are also normally held in libraries and the Citizens Advice Bureau. If the police gather information, for example when questioning a suspect, in a way that breaks these guidelines, a judge or magistrate may decide that such evidence cannot be used in court. The police officers concerned may also face disciplinary proceedings.

POWERS TO STOP

Police officers are entitled to stop and question any member of the public from whom they feel useful information about a crime can be obtained. However, the *Codes of Practice* emphasise the need for officers to behave responsibly, and say that they may be called upon to justify the use of such powers to a senior officer and in court.

Anyone who is stopped by a police officer may ask the officer's name and the police station where he or she works. They are also entitled to know why the officer has stopped them. It is not acceptable for this to be simply because of their colour, dress, hairstyle or the fact that they might have been in trouble before.

Strictly speaking, a member of the public does not have to answer an officer's questions. But a person's refusal to give, for example, their name and address, is likely to lead the officer to believe that the person has something significant to hide and therefore to make an arrest. It is an offence, which may lead to a fine or imprisonment, to mislead the police deliberately by giving false information or wasting their time.

Someone who is stopped by the police on suspicion that they have committed (or are about to commit) an *arrestable offence* - such as theft, assault or carrying an offensive weapon - should give their name and address, but need say no more. They have the right not to answer any more questions until they have received legal advice (see below).

POLICE

POWERS TO SEARCH

People

The police do not have the power to search anyone they choose, but they can carry out a search of someone (and the vehicle in which they are travelling) who has been arrested or is suspected of carrying:

- illegal drugs;
- stolen goods or goods on which duty has not been paid;
- weapons, or anything that might be used as a weapon; or
- anything that might be used for theft, burglary, deception, joyriding or the hunting or poaching of animals.

Before undertaking the search, the officer should give his or her name, explain why the search is taking place and state what he or she expects to find.

Searches carried out by the police in public should be restricted to an examination of a person's *outer* clothing. A search that requires more than the removal of an outer coat or jacket should be made out of public view, or in a police station or van, and should be done by someone of the same sex. The way the search is carried out can depend on what the police are looking for. For example the police may decide to carry out an intimate search of someone suspected of carrying drugs, given that people have been known to hide drugs inside their body.

Special powers

Police powers of search in certain circumstances have been extended by the *Criminal Justice and Public Order Act 1994*. If a senior police officer believes that a serious violent

incident might take place in the area, he or she can give officers the authority to stop *any* person or vehicle to search for offensive weapons or dangerous instruments. This applies even when the constable has no reasonable grounds for suspecting that the person stopped might have broken the law.

Anyone stopped in this way is entitled to a written record of the search. Failing to stop when asked by a police officer can result in a fine or imprisonment.

CITIZENSHIP
FOUNDATION

POLICE

Property

The police do not have the power to enter and search any house or building that they choose. But they are allowed to carry out a search if:
• they have the agreement of the occupier of the building; or
• they have reason to believe they might find someone who has committed an *arrestable offence*, or want to look for evidence in a property that was occupied by someone before they were arrested; or
• they have a warrant from a court; or
• they intend to catch an escaped prisoner, save life, prevent serious property damage or prevent some kind of disturbance.

If possible, the police should explain why they are making the search, and should keep a record of whether they needed to use force to get in, any damage caused, and whether they took anything away.

Arrest

When a police officer makes an arrest, he or she takes that person under the care and control of the law. This means that for the time being, they lose certain freedoms, but are, in return, given certain rights, designed to protect them against unreasonable treatment.

As soon as a person is arrested, they have the right to know why the police officer has taken this action. At the police station they are entitled to:
• see a solicitor (see below);
• have someone told where they are; and
• read a copy of the *Codes of Practice*, explaining the procedures the police should follow when taking someone into custody.

Anyone detained should be given a written note of these rights and cautioned. For the wording of this, see page 159.

The police may detain a member of the public if they do not have enough evidence to charge that person, but have good reason to believe that they can obtain further evidence by continuing with their detention.

A person cannot normally be held for more than 24 hours without being charged or released. If a serious offence is being investigated, a senior police officer can authorise detention for a further 12 hours, which can be extended up to a total of 96 hours, but only with the approval of a magistrates' court.

Helping the police with their enquiries

If you are asked to go to a police station to help with enquiries, it's important to know whether you are being arrested, or whether the decision to attend is up to you. If you are being asked to go voluntarily, you may refuse - although the police may then decide to arrest you - and then you have to go.

You have the right to send a message to your family or a friend telling them where you are, and to receive free legal advice from a solicitor, even though you are attending the police station voluntarily.

A person who has not been arrested, but goes to the police station voluntarily, may leave at any time they wish.

Questioning

There are clear rules governing the ways in which police officers can question a person, designed to stop unfair pressure being placed on a suspect. There should be regular breaks for food and comfort, the cell and interview room should be clean and properly heated, and the police should not follow a line of questioning that puts unreasonable pressure on the suspect. Someone who is deaf or has difficulty in understanding English should be provided with an interpreter. A doctor should be called to see a suspect who appears to be in need of medical treatment.

As soon as a police officer has reason to believe that the person being questioned has committed an offence (even if they have not been arrested), the officer must issue a caution. A few years ago, the wording of the police caution was changed. Today, a police officer will state: *"You do not have to say anything. But it may harm your defence if you do not mention when questioned something which you later rely on in court. Anything you do say may be given in evidence."*

At the police station a file is opened by the custody officer in which everything that happens to the suspect while at the station is recorded. The custody officer must repeat the caution and explain the suspect's right to consult a solicitor before answering further questions.

After giving his or her name and address, the suspect has the right to stay silent or to refuse to

CITIZENSHIP FOUNDATION

POLICE

answer certain further questions. However, if the case goes to trial, the court will be told of this and allowed, as the law says, "to draw such inferences as appear proper" if the suspect fails or refuses to:

• account for objects, substances or marks in or on their clothing or person at the time of their arrest;

• explain, after they have been arrested, where they were at the time the offence is alleged to have taken place; or

• mention something before they were charged, which they later rely on in their defence, or which it would have been reasonable to mention at the time.

If a police officer suspects that a person is mentally incapable of understanding the significance of the questions put to them, then an *appropriate adult* should be brought in to safeguard that person's rights. This would normally be a relative, friend, carer or an approved social worker. It may not be someone employed by the police. A similar safeguard is applied to interviews of anyone aged 16 or under.

Fingerprints, photographs and identification parades

The police can take the fingerprints of any person over the age of ten whom they have reason to suspect has been involved in a crime. If the person does not consent, reasonable force may be used.

The police may take photographs of anyone charged with a recordable offence. However, if the suspect refuses, force cannot be used. Both fingerprints and photographs must be destroyed if the person is not prosecuted for the offence or is charged, but acquitted.

A suspect cannot be made to take part in an identification parade, but his or her refusal can be given in evidence in court. Parades consist of at least eight people (in addition to the suspect) who must appear to resemble the suspect in age, height and general appearance. Normally only one suspect is included in each parade. The suspect may select his or her own position in the line. Witnesses are told that the suspect may or may not be in the line and witnesses are not under any obligation to identify someone. It is important to take legal advice if you are a suspect and are asked to take part in an identification parade.

MASTER
1. 2. 3.
LEFT
thumb
ID:314406/

THE LEGAL SYSTEM

Tape recording

Interviews at a police station are now normally recorded on tape. They begin with basic questions - name, address etc. - before moving on to more serious matters. If the interview is not recorded, notes should be made at the time by the interviewing officer. At the end of the interview the suspect and his or her lawyer should be shown the transcript, asked to indicate any inaccuracies and to sign it as a fair record of what was said.

Assessing the evidence

After questioning a suspect, the police must then decide what to do next. If there appears to be enough evidence, they can charge the person with the offence and send the papers to the Crown Prosecution Service which will review the file and decide whether to go ahead with the prosecution.

In some situations the police will issue a formal caution. This is a strong warning from a senior police officer reminding the person that they could have been sent to court, and that if they commit further offences, that is almost certainly what will happen. Formal cautions are given more often now because the re-offence rate is lower among those who do not go to court. Cautions, however, cannot be given for serious offences or if the person refuses to admit their guilt.

If the police feel there is not enough evidence to make a charge, they will either decide to take no further action (and the case will be dropped), or will delay any decision while further enquiries are made.

Criminal responsibility

Generally a child under ten who breaks the law is not charged with the crime. It's felt that children under this age are usually too young  to weigh up what is right and wrong and deliberately break the law. However, children under ten who are out of control can be taken into care by a local authority.

Any person who appears to be mentally disordered or unable to understand the significance of questions that are being put to them should be given special consideration if suspected or accused of a crime. Definitions and details of this are given in the *Mental Health Act 1983* and in the *Codes of Practice* for the *Police and Criminal Evidence Act 1984*, see page 156.

LEGAL ADVICE AT A POLICE STATION

In almost all circumstances, anyone who is being questioned at a police station (whether attending voluntarily or under arrest) will be informed by the police of their right to see or speak in private to a duty solicitor or another solicitor of their choice. The consultation with the solicitor is free and in private.

If someone has been arrested, is being questioned about a serious arrestable offence, or feels unsure about their legal position, it is better for them not to answer questions (except their name and address) until they have had a chance to speak to a solicitor.

When the police are investigating a very serious offence they can, with the approval of a senior officer, delay access to a solicitor on the grounds that talking to a solicitor might interfere with the evidence, alert other suspects or hinder the recovery of stolen property.

BAIL

Someone charged with an offence should normally be released on bail - unless the police or court feel that there is a real risk in doing so. Bail may be refused, for example, if there is doubt over the name and address of the suspect or defendant, if there is concern for their safety or that of others, or if it is felt that the suspect or defendant may fail to attend court when next required.

If the police do not allow bail, the suspect or defendant must be brought before a magistrate at the earliest opportunity, who will decide whether he or she can be released on bail, and if so what conditions should apply.

Bail cannot be given to anyone charged with murder, attempted murder, rape or attempted rape who already has a conviction for one of these offences.

Courts also need not grant bail if it appears that the defendant was already on bail when the offence was committed.

COMPLAINTS AGAINST THE POLICE

If you feel you have suffered, or witnessed, police misconduct, you may decide to make an official complaint. This should be done within one year of the incident.

Try to obtain as many details as you can about the incident and those involved. It usually helps to make a note of what happened as soon as you can. It's also important to be clear about exactly why you feel the officer's behaviour was unacceptable. If you are complaining about a relatively serious matter, it is a good idea to speak to a solicitor or contact the Citizens Advice Bureau beforehand.

You may make your complaint in person, at the police station, or put it in writing for the attention of the Chief Constable of the police force concerned. In London, it should be addressed to the Metropolitan Police Commissioner. If you wish, it is possible for someone else, for example the Citizens Advice Bureau, to make the complaint on your behalf, although you will need to give them written consent to do so.

All recorded complaints against the police are investigated and the investigation is overseen by an officer of the rank of chief inspector or above. Although there is no set procedure, he or she will seek views of the incident from yourself, the officer concerned, and any other significant witnesses. If your complaint is found to be valid, you may receive an apology from the investigating officer or the Chief Constable. If you are unhappy with this, you may ask for the matter to be passed to the *Police Complaints Authority*, although this is unlikely to be accepted if the complaint was only over a minor issue.

Complaints over serious matters, and in particular those alleging that the conduct of the police officer resulted in actual bodily harm, serious injury or death, are automatically referred to the Police Complaints Authority. This is a civilian body made up of people who have never been members of the police. The investigation will be carried out at a formal level and may result in disciplinary action or referral of the case to the Director of

COURTS

Public Prosecutions, if the officer has committed a criminal offence.

If you have a serious complaint against the police, it is important to take legal advice from a solicitor, law centre or Citizens Advice Bureau. Further information on the procedures involved can be obtained from the Police Complaints Authority, see **Contacts** for details.

Complaints or concerns about police *policy* in your area are best drawn to the attention of your MP or local councillor, or to the police through their consultative or public liaison committees. Your local police station will be able to suggest the most appropriate channels to go through.

COURTS

The Court Service publishes a *Charter for Court Users* outlining the support and services you can expect if you ever need to attend a Crown or county court. It explains, for example, that it is possible for someone due to appear as a witness in a case to visit a courtroom before the case starts in order

to become more familiar with the layout and for an extra seat to be available for anyone accompanying them.

The Charter also outlines the work of all the main courts (except the magistrates' courts) and gives details of the procedure to be followed if you have a complaint about the handling of a case by the court staff. Copies are available from the Customer Service Unit, tel 0171 210 2269. Complaints relating to magistrates' courts should be made to the Justices Chief Executive of the magistrates' court committee for the area.

LEGAL ADVICE AT COURT

Although it preferable to see a solicitor before going to court, in many circumstances the defendant is entitled to free legal advice on their first appearance at a magistrates' court. The duty solicitor can advise the defendant on applying for bail, whether to plead guilty or not guilty, the possible sentence and how to obtain further legal advice. Except in limited cases, the duty solicitor can also represent the client when he or she first appears in front of the magistrates.

JURY SERVICE

The task of the twelve members of a jury in the Crown Court is to decide on the facts of a criminal case and on whether the defendant is guilty of the offence. Anyone aged between 18 and 70 whose name appears on the Electoral Register and who has lived in Britain for a continuous period of five years, from the age of 13, is liable to be called for service. However, anyone aged 65 or over is excused of right, although they must attend if they have not asked to be excused.

There are certain categories of people who are disqualified from jury service. These include members of the legal profession, prison officers and governors, probation officers, police officers and ministers of religion. Neither judges nor magistrates may serve on a jury, either during or after their term of office. Also ineligible are those on bail and those who have been on probation within the last five years or sentenced to prison or community service within the last ten. It is an offence to serve on a jury knowing you are not qualified to do so.

You will usually be given at least four weeks notice if you are called for jury service. Although some people, such as MPs and members of the medical profession have the right to be excused, normally it is compulsory. If there is a strong reason why you are unable to serve - such as the care of a relative or a holiday that has already been booked - then you can apply to be excused, or have your service deferred, although it is important to make this clear as soon as possible.

You will be given information about what you are expected to do and may be shown a short video about trial procedure at the beginning of your period of service. You can claim the cost of meals and travel to Court together with a daily allowance for any loss of earnings, or other financial loss.

CITIZENSHIP FOUNDATION

COURTS

The words they use

Barristers	A lawyer who works on instructions from a prosecution or defence solicitor and represents people in court in more serious cases. Barristers often specialise in particular areas of law and are consulted by solicitors for advice.
County Court	Where all but the most complicated civil cases are dealt with. These most commonly include claims for debt, personal injury, breach of contract, repossession of a house, divorce and adoption proceedings.
Court of Appeal	Appeals against convictions and sentences by the Crown Court and against decisions in county courts and the High Court are dealt with by the Court of Appeal.
Crown Court	The criminal court where serious (or *indictable*) offences are heard. The job of the judge is to make sure that the evidence is properly presented and to rule on matters of law. It is members of the jury who decide the verdict. If the defendant is found guilty, the judge will pass sentence.
Crown Prosecution Service (CPS)	The process of investigating a crime and then charging a suspect is undertaken by the police, but it is the CPS which decides which cases are prosecuted. The CPS is an independent prosecuting service, made up of Crown Prosecutors, who decide whether there is a realistic chance of conviction and whether the crime is so serious as to merit a trial. If the answer to either of these questions is "no", the case will be dropped. It is difficult to predict the length of time required for the investigation and prosecution of any offences. If you are charged with a less serious offence, which would normally be heard in a magistrates' court, you should know within six months whether you are to be prosecuted.

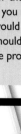

COURTS

The words they use

High Court	Most of the civil cases not dealt with by the county courts are heard at the Royal Courts of Justice or at one of the High Court centres in England and Wales.
Magistrate's court	Proceedings for all criminal cases begin in the magistrates' court. Those involving less serious (or *summary*) offences are heard by magistrates in full. More serious cases, involving *indictable* offences, are passed by magistrates to the Crown Court if they are satisfied that there is enough evidence to justify committing the defendant for trial or the defendant chooses to be tried before a jury. Normally, cases are heard by three magistrates (also called justices of the peace), who are unpaid members of the local community.
Solicitors	Lawyers trained to provide legal advice, to take action on your behalf and to represent you in court or at a tribunal (although they may engage a barrister to represent their client in higher courts and to give specialist advice).
Tribunals	Informal courts dealing with matters of civil law. Separate tribunals deal with questions of employment, immigration, rent, social security, pensions and mental health.
Youth court	Criminal cases involving young people below the age of 18 are normally heard in a youth court. However, a young person charged jointly with an adult can be sent for trial at the magistrates' court or Crown Court. When a young person is charged with murder or certain other grave offences, the trial will be held in a Crown Court. Members of the public are not normally allowed in court to listen to the case, nor can the name or identity of the young person accused be reported in the press. However the court may allow the name of a young person who has been convicted to be published, if it considers this is in the public interest.

INFORMATION AND LEGAL ADVICE

THE CITIZENS ADVICE BUREAU

Usually known as the CAB, the Citizens Advice Bureau gives free, confidential and independent information and advice on all kinds of problems. Enquiries can be made by 'phone or in person at any of their offices, found in almost every town and city in England and Wales. Opening hours vary, so, if you intend to visit, it is worth checking beforehand. The number will be in the local telephone directory. CABs are able to help with making 'phone calls, writing letters, helping to prepare cases and even providing representation at tribunals. They can also suggest the names of local solicitors who specialise in the type of case with which you are concerned

LAW CENTRES

There are 52 Law Centres in England and Wales which are able to provide legal advice and represent individuals in legal proceedings. Most are located in London and the north of England, with very few in the south and one Centre in Wales (Cardiff).

and also those who offer a free or fixed-fee initial interview.

Some CABs also have a solicitor and other specialists available to give free advice, for example, on one evening a week.

SOLICITORS
Choosing a solicitor

No solicitor is experienced in every area of law. Quite often firms specialise in a limited number of areas, such as housing, immigration or employment law, which means that it can take some time to find the right local solicitor for your needs.

You can get the names of all the local firms of solicitors from the Citizens Advice Bureau, together with an indication of the kind of work in which they specialise. They can also tell you which firms offer legal aid. Main libraries also hold copies of the Solicitors' Regional Directory, which shows the types of work done by of every firm of solicitors in the country.

Local courts can also be useful. Although they may not recommend individual firms, they may give you the names of two or three local firms regularly doing the work in which you are interested.

INFORMATION AND LEGAL ADVICE

Information

When you telephone the solicitor's office, explain the problem and the kind of service you need. You should not have to wait more than a week for an appointment. If you have difficulty in getting to the office, it's worth asking if they can arrange a home visit.

It's usually helpful to take some time to prepare for the first appointment - collecting together papers or other information with a bearing on your case. Make sure you're clear about what you want to say to the solicitor and what you need to know in return. It saves time to make a note of these points beforehand.

At the end of the first interview you should know how your solicitor sees the problem, the options that are open to you, the amount of time that everything is likely to take and what it is likely to cost.

If the case proceeds, the solicitor should keep you informed of all developments - even if there aren't any. You should also be told if your case is taken over or being handled by someone else.

Costs

Solicitors usually charge according to the amount of time they spend on the work, including letters and telephone calls to you. You may wish to agree an upper limit for the bill, which the solicitor should not exceed without first checking with you. You may ask to have regular bills sent to you as the work progresses. Solicitors are quite entitled to ask for part payment in advance. Your solicitor should also explain the likelihood of your having to meet other costs - including the payment of the other side's legal fees, as well as your own - and must tell you if you are eligible for legal aid.

Complaints

If you have a complaint about any of the work that is being done, it's usually best to raise it first with the solicitor concerned or the partner in the firm designated to deal with complaints. (The firm's own formal complaints procedure should have been explained to you at your first meeting with the solicitor.)

The *Office for the Supervision of Solicitors* produces a special Complaint Resolution Form

INFORMATION AND LEGAL ADVICE

which you can use to outline your concern for forwarding to the solicitor. Copies are available from your solicitor, the Citizens Advice Bureau and the Office for the Supervision of Solicitors (OSS) itself. See **Contacts**.

If you remain dissatisfied, then get in touch with the OSS through their Helpline, and they will send you further information together with a Complaint Referral Form on which you explain the nature of your complaint and what you are hoping to achieve. When they have received this, the OSS will either refer the complaint back to the solicitor, help you and your solicitor resolve the problem or carry out an investigation themselves. The OSS has the power to reduce the solicitor's bill, order the solicitor to pay compensation of up to £1,000, require the solicitor to correct the mistake at his or her own expense or to discipline the solicitor for misconduct.

LEGAL AID

Although the cost of legal advice and representation can be very high, there are various ways in which you may be able to obtain low-cost initial advice and to have some of your costs reduced through help from legal aid.

Those firms of solicitors which undertake legal aid work display the Legal Aid logo at their premises. Some will be franchised firms, specially approved by the Legal Aid Board for their standards and quality of service. To find a Legal Aid franchised firm in your area, call free on 0500 282 300.

Low-cost interviews

Some solicitors are prepared to give an initial free or low-cost interview which should help you understand your legal position more clearly. Quite often, firms offering this service advertise in the local paper or Yellow Pages. The Citizens Advice Bureau should also be able to give you further details.

Legal advice and assistance scheme

This was previously known as the *Green Form scheme* but the green application form is being phased out. It pays for up to two hours free advice and assistance from a solicitor. Three hours

THE LEGAL SYSTEM

work is available for matrimonial cases involving the preparation of a divorce petition. Help from the solicitor can include written and spoken advice, writing letters, filling in forms, negotiating a settlement or assistance with preparing a case for a court or tribunal.

Help with most issues is available through the *advice and assistance scheme* - although it doesn't usually cover making a will or the purchase or sale of property. However free advice on drawing up a will is available to anyone aged 70 or over, or to anyone who is blind, deaf or without speech, or who suffers any other substantial, permanent disability.

The scheme is means tested, with limits placed on disposable income and capital. Anyone receiving Income Support, income-based Job Seeker's Allowance, Family Credit or Disability Working Allowance will qualify, depending on their level of capital. For someone without dependents, the capital limit is £1,000. The application for legal advice and assistance is made through a solicitor, who will be able to tell you at once whether or not you qualify.

Any money recovered as a result of legal advice and assistance must be used by the solicitor to pay his or her bill.

Assistance by Way of Representation

This scheme, usually known as ABWOR, covers the cost of a solicitor preparing a case and representing the client in most civil cases in the magistrates' court. It is available for cases involving separation, maintenance, paternity and defended adoption proceedings, to patients appearing before Mental Health Review Tribunals, to prisoners facing disciplinary charges and to life prisoners whose cases are referred to the Parole Board.

Like the *advice and assistance scheme*, ABWOR is means tested, although there is no means test for Mental Health Review Tribunal cases when ABWOR for legal representation is provided free of charge. Applications are again made through a solicitor.

Applicants may have to pay a contribution towards the cost of ABWOR and any money recovered must be put towards paying the solicitor's bill.

INFORMATION AND LEGAL ADVICE

Civil Legal Aid

Civil Legal Aid can pay for some or all of the costs of preparing and taking a case to court, including representation by a solicitor and, if necessary, a barrister. Like the other forms of legal aid, it is means tested, with limits set for income and capital. Many people today are outside these limits and do not qualify, although anyone on Income Support, Family Credit or income-based Jobseekers Allowance automatically qualifies.

Civil Legal Aid is not available for certain kinds of cases. The Government is proposing that *conditional fee agreements* (see below) could replace legal aid in personal injury cases (excluding medical negligence), disputes over inheritance, boundaries, business trusts, company law and partnership matters.

Legal aid applications for cases involving relatively small amounts of money or with little chance of success are not usually granted. Applications for Civil Legal Aid are made through a solicitor who is also able to advise on the likelihood of qualifying.

Again, the legal aid office

will deduct from any money awarded by the court as much as may be needed to cover the legal costs.

No win no fee

It is now possible in personal injury and, in certain other cases, for the payment of a solicitor's fee to depend on whether the case is won or lost.

It is up to the solicitor to decide whether to take a case on this basis (because of the risk of getting nothing). If the solicitor does take the case, he or she will be entitled to charge up to double the fees normally payable out of your damages. The percentage uplift, as it is called, has to be negotiated at the start and it's a good idea to compare two firm's proposals. If you can, use a solicitor you trust will make a fair uplift.

"No win, no fee" cases need careful consideration. You will usually be liable for the expenses (court fees, witnesses and costs etc.) and, if you lose, all the lawyers' costs and expenses of the other side. Sometimes you can insure against these risks, but this is likely to be expensive and needs good advice from your solicitor. The final shape of the "no win, no fee" scheme is still

GOVERNMENT

PARLIAMENT

COURTS

EUROPEAN LAW

ELECTIONS

COMPLAINTS

CHARTERS

MAKING THE LAW

PARLIAMENT

Between 50-60 new laws are passed by Parliament each year. Known initially as a Bill, each one is debated and voted on by the House of Commons and the House of Lords before becoming law. The House of Lords can comment on a Bill and recommend changes, but it can't actually stop it from being passed. The only Bill that the House of Lords can reject is one from the Commons which tries to extend Parliament beyond five years (the maximum time between general elections) - a protection against power being seized by a dictator.

In 1999 or 2000 the Government is likely to begin a long process of reforming the House of Lords, which will include legislation to remove hereditary peers from Parliament.

After going through both Houses of Parliament, a Bill is given the royal assent by the Queen. Today this is just a formality. The last monarch to refuse to approve an Act was Queen Anne in 1707.

Most Bills are put to Parliament by the Government as part of its overall policy, although a small number are presented by individual MPs and Peers. These are known as private members' Bills. Few of these become law, as there is only a limited amount of time to debate and vote on them. Most of Parliament's time is spent on Government business.

THE NATIONAL ASSEMBLY FOR WALES

Following the referendum held in September 1997, the Government introduced the *Government of Wales Bill* setting out the proposed structure for a new Welsh Assembly, likely to be established in 1999. The Assembly will consist of 60 members, elected every four years.

Wales will remain an integral part of the United Kingdom and will continue to share a common legal system with England. The framework of all laws for Wales will still be passed by Parliament in London, although the Assembly will be able to influence issues being considered in Westminster which could

GOVERNMENT

affect Wales. The Secretary of State for Wales will also have a duty to consult the Assembly about the Government's legislative programme after it has been announced in the Queen's Speech.

PAPER GWYN
Llais dros Gymru

Cynigion y Llywodraeth ar gyfer Cynulliad Cymreig

cases are dealt with in a consistent way. However, there are times when a particular set of circumstances may never have arisen before, or when a judge decides that existing judgments are no longer in tune with modern society. In these situations, by their decision, judges can create or change the law.

The Assembly will have responsibility for devising the Orders, rules and regulations, outlining how legislation will be implemented in Wales - within areas such as education, health, industry, agriculture, transport, training and environment. Matters of foreign affairs, defence, taxation, social security and broadcasting will continue to be decided on a common basis throughout the United Kingdom.

COURTS

When a case comes to court, the magistrates or judge must usually deal with it according to the same principles as courts have done in the past. This system of *precedent* ensures that similar

A month after separating from his wife, a man broke into her parents' house, where she was staying, and tried to have sexual intercourse with her, against her will. The husband pleaded guilty to attempted rape and was sentenced to five years imprisonment. He appealed against this sentence on the grounds that a husband could not be found guilty of raping his wife. The case moved to the Court of Appeal and then to the House of Lords, where it was heard by five of the most senior judges in the country. They decided that the ruling which said that a husband could not be found guilty of raping his wife (which went back to before 1736) should no longer form part of the law, since husbands and wives should be seen as equal partners in marriage. As a result, the law was changed. A man who forces his wife to have sexual intercourse against her will can now be found guilty of rape.

EUROPEAN LAW

Britain is one of 15 member states of the European Union (EU). The EU's powers are those that have been given to it by the member states through the treaties that they have signed. These extend to many areas of life, including transport, agriculture, civil liberties, women's rights and the environment. However there are others - such as criminal justice, property rights, education and social security - where the EU has no power.

The *Council of Ministers*, made up of government ministers from each member state, decides on actions that need to be taken at European level.

The *European Commission* makes proposals on how these measures might be achieved. It comprises 20 Commissioners, appointed by national governments for a period of five years. The European Commission also makes sure that member states respect the rules,

once they have been agreed.

The proposals made by the European Commission are then generally examined by the *European Parliament*. This is a democratically elected body with members (MEPs) elected directly from each of the member states every five years. It has growing influence on the process of legislation and the EU's budget (although over some areas of expenditure, including the Common Agricultural Policy, the Council of Ministers has the final say).

The *European Court of Justice*, is responsible for ensuring that Community law is observed. It can be asked to interpret Community law in cases referred to it by national courts and can review the legality of certain acts of the Council and Commission.

The European Convention on Human Rights

The Convention came into force in 1953 and sets out a number of fundamental political and civil rights, including the right to liberty, the right to a fair trial, respect for private and family life, freedom of thought, conscience and religion.

Many European countries have legal systems which give international treaties, such as the

Convention, the status of domestic law once they are ratified and some others have incorporated the Convention rights into their own legal system.

The United Kingdom has not incorporated the Convention, but the *Human Rights Bill*, which was introduced to Parliament in October 1997, will require all legislation to be interpreted, so far as is possible, in accordance with the Convention rights and for public authorities to act in a way which is compatible with the rights. The Bill is likely to receive the royal assent in 1998, but it will be some time after this before the main provisions come into force, because of the need to train judges, magistrates and tribunal members.

REGISTERING TO VOTE

In October of each year, an electoral registration form is delivered to every household in the country. The form should be completed by the head of the household, with details of everyone resident, aged 16 years and over.

You can check if your name, or anyone else's, is on the Electoral Register at your local main library or council offices.

Mrs Day, who worked 1 hours a week part-time as a cleaner, did not receive any redundancy pay when she was made redundant by Hertfordshire County Council. This was because unde British law redundancy pay was available only to those working for 16 or more hours a week. Mrs Day thought this was unfai and, with help from the Equal Opportunities Commission, took her case to Court. The case reached the House of Lords where three senior judges decided that, by denying employment protection rights to part time workers, British law was discriminating against women - who made up the bulk of the part-time workforce. The judges said that this broke an important principle o European law which says that men and women should be treated equally. As a result, the law was changed by Parliament, giving employment protection rights to all workers, whether full or part-time - and, in this area bringing British and European law into line

VOTING AND ELECTIONS

VOTING

Voters must be 18 or over on the day of the election and have their name on the Electoral Register. There is a long list of categories of people eligible to vote in local government, British and European Parliamentary elections. These include British citizens, citizens of the Republic of Ireland, Commonwealth citizens, British Nationals (Overseas), British Overseas citizens, British Dependent Territories citizens and British subjects. Citizens of the European Union living here may vote in elections for the European Parliament and local government, but not the British Parliament, provided their names are on the Electoral Register.

Those unable to vote in Parliamentary elections include members of the House of Lords, anyone convicted of corrupt practices at an election during the previous five years and anyone who is being compulsorily held for treatment of a mental illness (although the rights of people in this last category are not absolutely clear, see below). The only prisoners eligible to vote are those on remand, those convicted and not sentenced, and those transferred to psychiatric care in a hospital, by order of the Home Secretary during their sentence.

Hospital and residential care

Anyone in hospital when the Electoral Register is being drawn up should be registered at their normal home address. People receiving long term care are normally registered at the residential or nursing home where they are staying.

Mental Illness

Patients who are voluntarily receiving short term psychiatric care in hospital can register to vote in the normal way - using their home address for registration. Those in long term voluntary care can register by completing a *patient's declaration form*, using their usual or last address - but not that of the hospital. The hospital can provide this form.

Generally speaking, patients who are compulsorily detained in hospital lose the right to vote in an election because they no longer

VOTING AND ELECTIONS

have an address to which they are free to return. However, this ruling has been challenged by the mental health charity MIND, because a detained patient may, in certain circumstances, continue to have a place of residence outside the hospital. The latest Home Office guidance acknowledges this - and it is now possible for someone who was detained shortly before the registration date to register as an elector. But anyone detained in hospital more than six months before the registration date would find it difficult to claim to be resident at their own home and, as a result, would be unable to register to vote.

Postal and proxy voting

Anyone who is eligible to vote, but unable to attend the polling station in person, may apply for a postal or proxy vote. Postal votes are available to people in a range of situations, for example, in hospital, on holiday or away from home through work.

Someone, unable to vote in person, because of poor eyesight or another physical disability, can apply to the registration officer to be placed on a list of absent voters and

to receive a postal vote. This facility is also available to carers.

A vote by proxy is made by arranging for someone else to vote in the way that you want, on your behalf.

Electors who are unable to read may ask the presiding officer to mark their ballot paper with their vote - but they must be able to state how they wish to vote and cannot use the help of a relative or carer. Voters who are blind, however, are entitled to have help from a companion. For further details contact the Electoral Registration Department of your local council.

ELECTIONS
Local Elections

The election of local councillors is held every four years, usually in the first week of May - although not all councils hold them in the same year.

In most areas, there are three levels of local government - county, district or town, and parish or community councils. In London, the local councils are the 32 Boroughs. In other major cities, it is usually the unitary authority and metropolitan districts that carry out the principal local government work.

Between them, and sometimes

CITIZENSHIP
FOUNDATION

in conjunction with national government, these councils are responsible for education, planning, refuse, environment, recreation, passenger transport, libraries, children's homes, council housing and car parks.

General elections

The election of all MPs (there are currently 659 in the UK, and 569 of these in England and Wales) must take place at least every five years. Often, however, the party in power will call an election before this if it feels it will help its chances of gaining a further term of office or, more rarely, because it has been defeated on a vital vote in

the House of Commons and has lost the confidence of the House.

If an MP dies or resigns, a by-election takes place to elect a new MP for that constituency.

Almost all MPs represent a political party and the party, with the greatest number of MPs forms the Government, with the party leader becoming Prime Minister. In 1997 the new government announced a programme of political reform which included a proposal to hold a referendum on our current voting system and whether, in particular, to introduce a system of proportional representation.

European elections

At European elections we elect representatives to the European Parliament based in Strasbourg, France. These take place every 5 years. The next Euro-elections will be in 1999.

There are 87 Euro-constituencies in the UK (76 of these in England and Wales). Most candidates belong to one of the main political parties and, if elected, join the MEPs of the 14 other countries currently forming the European Union. It is inevitable that, from time to time, the actions of public bodies (councils, hospitals,

Councillor, MP or MEP?

A person can stand for political office from the age of 21. Candidates for the local council must either:

- have their name on the local electoral roll; or
- rent or own land or property or have worked in the area for the last 12 months; or
- have lived within three miles of the area for the last 12 months.

These rules do not apply to candidates for Parliamentary or European elections. Someone standing as an MP must put up a deposit of £500, which they lose if they get less than 5% of the votes cast. The deposit for prospective European Parliamentary candidates is £1,000, likely to be increased to £5,000 by the end of 1998.

social security offices etc.), do not meet with everyone's approval. In these circumstances, you may wish to influence or alter a decision, or simply gain further information about a particular issue. Some of the details, and particularly the organisations (see **Contacts**), mentioned in this book may be of help, as may the local Citizens Advice Bureau and library. Larger public libraries are now beginning to offer the public access to the internet (although this is by no means widespread), and also carry detailed notes produced by the Citizens Advice Bureau on a huge range of topics, which are normally available for anyone to read and use.

ACCESS TO GOVERNMENT INFORMATION

Government departments are now committed to be more open in their dealings with members of the public. Although some categories of information relating to defence and law enforcement may not be released, the *Code of Practice on Access to Government Information* gives a commitment to provide the facts and reasoning behind major policy decisions and to reveal internal guidelines about departments' dealings with the public. Most information is available free and government bodies are expected to respond to requests for information within a period of 20 working days. To obtain a copy of the Code of Practice, see **Contacts** for details.

It is the Government's intention to introduce a *Freedom of Information Act* in 1999 or 2000, giving everyone the right to see information held by national, regional and local government and some organisations working on behalf of government.

COMPLAINTS

Public services normally have established procedures for dealing with complaints.

Whoever you are dealing with, it will generally be more effective if you:

- act as quickly as possible;
- think carefully about what you want to achieve and, if necessary, obtain advice;
- make sure you talk or write to

Citizen's Charters

National charters cover the key public services, such as the courts, the National Health Service and the Benefits Agency. They set out the standards of service that people can expect and how to complain if things go wrong.

There are also charters covering local services, such as individual GP practices, local hospitals, schools and community care services.

Copies of charters are free and are normally available from the organisation concerned. The Citizen's Charter Publication Line, tel 0345 22 32 42 (calls charged at local rates) can tell you how to get a copy of any of the national charters.

If you feel a public organisation, such as a school, hospital or library, is providing an excellent service, you can nominate it for a Charter Mark by telephoning 0645 400 444 (local rates). See **Contacts** for details.

a person - such as the manager or director of services - who has the authority to deal with your complaint;

• find out the name of the person you are talking to;

• stick to the facts, state clearly what you want to be done, set a reasonable time within which this should happen, and get back in touch if they haven't met the deadline; and

• keep a record of 'phone calls or letters that you send.

The Ombudsman

If you are still unhappy with the way a problem has been handled by a government department or public service, you may take your case to an Ombudsman (the word is taken from the Swedish, meaning a senior government official).

The Parliamentary Ombudsman deals with complaints from members of the public over mal-administration by government departments and agencies. Typical problems include unnecessary delay, failure to follow the correct procedures, discourtesy, misleading advice and mistakes in handling claims. The Ombudsman also deals with complaints of difficulty in obtaining access to

official information.
Ombudsman services are free to members of the public and are completely independent.

Before a complaint can be reported to the Parliamentary Ombudsman, as much as possible must have been done to sort out the problem with the depart-ment or body concerned, and all the usual channels of enquiry and grievance procedures must have been exhausted.

If you want to complain to the Ombudsman, you should write to, or go and see, an MP - it need not be your local one - through whom applications to the Ombudsman must be made. If the Ombudsman upholds your complaint, he or she will expect the organisation or department concerned to take appropriate action. This might include an apology, provision of the service requested, putting right what went wrong and, possibly, financial compensation.

It is important to draw a complaint to the attention of the Ombudsman as soon as possible. A Helpline is available giving guidance on the application procedure and the kind of cases the Parliamentary Ombudsman can consider, tel 0171 276 2130.

The Local Government Ombudsman investigates complaints about the administration of local government services. See **Contacts**.

Writing to your Councillor, MP or MEP

If your problem is local, contact your local councillor through the council office. MPs or MEPs can best take up problems for which the Government or European Union are responsible. Most MPs and some MEPs have local "surgeries", for which no appointment is necessary. These are often held on Saturdays, and advertised in the local paper. You can also write to your MEP locally and your MP at the House of Commons. Addresses are obtainable from your local library, and should also be listed under *Member of Parliament* in the business section of the 'phone book.

Judicial review

If a public body - such as a government department, local authority or hospital - makes a decision or takes action which actually seems to be against the law, it is possible to apply to have that decision reviewed or over-turned in the High Court. Known as judicial review, it's a way of having illegal or unreasonable decisions changed. For example, in the past, hospitals have been challenged on their refusal to undertake a particular operation, and action has been taken against the Home Office over its ruling to deport someone who was a British citizen.

A judicial review can be started only when all other avenues of complaint have been exhausted. Before doing anything, it's important to get advice from a solicitor who understands this area of law.

Age Concern (England) 1268 London Road, London SW16 4ER, tel 0181 679 8000 and Age Concern (Wales) 4th Floor, 1 Cathedral Road, Cardiff CF1 9SD, tel 01222 371 566, cares about all older people and finds effective ways to make later life fulfilling and enjoyable. Locally, a network of 1,400 groups and 250,000 volunteers provides community-based services such as lunch clubs, day centres and home visiting. Nationally, Age Concern campaigns on issues surrounding the subject of ageing, undertakes research, provides information and advice and offers a wide range of training.

Further information on many of the subjects covered in this book is available in the factsheet series, published by Age Concern. For a full list of factsheets call the freephone line 0800 00 99 66 or write to Age Concern, FREEPOST (SWB 30375), Ashburton, Devon TQ13 7ZZ.

Citizens Advice Bureau - usually known as the CAB - gives free, confidential and independent information and advice on all kinds of problems. You can make an enquiry by 'phone or go to one of their offices, found in almost every town and city. For your nearest CAB, see the local 'phone book.

Citizen's Charters - for details of how to obtain copies of all the charters, call the Citizen's Charter Publication Line, tel 0345 22 32 42 (calls charged at local rates). Disability Discrimination Information Line tel 0345 622 633

Disability Law Service, Part 2nd Floor North, High Holborn House, 52-54 High Holborn, London WC1V 6RL, tel 0171 831 8031. Able to advise and help disabled people, their family, friends and carers on a wide range of law-related subjects including work, housing, benefits and community care.

Free Representation Unit, 49-51 Bedford Row, London WC1R 4LR, tel 0171 831 0692. A charitable organisation of barristers and law students who will represent clients without charge at social security and industrial tribunals. However they will only take on cases referred to them by CABs, solicitors and law centres.

Law Centres Federation, Duchess House, 18-19 Warren Street, London W1P 5DB, tel 0171 387 8570, can give you the name and address of your nearest law centre.

Law Society, 113 Chancery Lane, London WC2A 1PL, tel 0171 242 1222, provides information on using a solicitor.

Liberty (National Council for Civil Liberties), 21 Tabbard Street, London SE1 4LA, tel 0171 403 3888. Liberty is a campaigning organisation able to answer queries by post, from people who feel their civil liberties have been infringed.

Saga Magazine is a source of valuable information and consumer advice. To subscribe, call 01303 711 526, or write to Saga Publishing Ltd., Freepost CU250, Folkestone, Kent CT20 1BR.

Health

Action for Victims of Medical Accidents, Bank Chambers, 1 London Road, Forest Hill, London SE23 3TP, tel 0181 291 2783.

British Society of Dentistry for the Handicapped, 6 Elizabeth Close, Henley on Thames, Oxfordshire.

Community Health Councils give advice to anyone who feels they have a complaint about any aspect of the health services. Found under "C" in the 'phone directory.

Health Information Service, a free confidential service, operating normal office hours, and able to give information on a wide variety of health matters, including local contacts and what to do if you are not happy with the treatment or service you have been given, tel 0800 66 55 44.

Health Service Ombudsman, Millbank Tower, London SW1P 4QP, tel 0171 217 4051, and (for Wales), 5th Floor, Capital Tower, Greyfriars Road, Cardiff CF1 3AG, tel 01222 394 621.

Mental Health Act Commission, Maid Marian House, 56 Hounds Gate, Nottingham NG1 6BG, tel 0115 943 7100.

MIND, Granta House, 15-19 Broadway, London E15 4BQ, tel 0181 519 2122. Information on all aspects of mental health. Mind Legal Advice Line Mon, Wed, Fri, 2-4.30pm, ext 299, or contact local regional offices

Patient's Association, PO Box 935, Harrow HA1 3YJ, tel 0181 423 9111. A helpline is also available, tel 0181 423 8999.

Terrence Higgins Trust, 52-54 Grays Inn Road, London WC1X 8JU, tel 0171 831 0330. A registered charity able to inform, advise and help on AIDS or HIV infection. A Helpline is open everyday, 12 noon - 10pm, tel 0171 242 1010. Legal advice, information and help is available on the Legal Line on Monday and Wednesday, between 7pm-9pm, tel 0171 405 2381.

Family

Animal Aid (organises the Humane Research Donor Card), The Old Chapel, Tonbridge, Kent TN9 1NL, tel 01732 364 546.

Funeral Ombudsman, 31 Southampton Row, London WC1B 5HJ, tel 0171 4301112.

Institute of Burials and Cremation Administration, tel 01636 708 311.

National Stepfamily Association, 3rd floor, Chapel House, 18 Hatton Place, London, EC1N 8RU, tel 0171 209 2460 can provide information and advice to any member of a stepfamily or anyone affected by stepfamilies. They also run a Helpline open Mon-Fri 2pm-5pm & 7pm-10pm operated by trained counsellors with experience of stepfamilies, tel 0990 168 388.

Organ Donor Register, administered by the UK Transplant Support Service Authority, Fox Den Road, Stoke Gifford, Bristol BS12 6RR, tel 0117 975 7575.

Principal Registry of the Family Division, 2nd floor, Somerset House, The Strand, London WC2 1LP, tel 0171 936 6000.

Woodland Trust, Autumn Park, Dysart Road, Grantham, Lincs NG31 6LL, tel 01476 74297

War Pensions Agency, a Helpline is open Mon-Thurs 8.15am-5.15pm and Fri 8.15am-4.30pm, tel 01253 858 858.

Women's Aid is able to provide information, support and advice for women experiencing domestic violence in the home. **Women's Aid England** run a Helpline, Mon-Thurs 10am-5pm and Fri 10am-3pm, tel 0345 023 468.
Welsh Women's Aid is open Mon-Fri 10.00-4.00pm, tel 01222 390 874 (Cardiff), 01970 612 748 (Aberystwyth), 01745 334 767 (Rhyl).

Home

Advice Information and Mediation Service for Retirement Housing, Walkden House, 3-10 Melton Street, London NW1 2EJ, tel 0171 383 2006.

Anchor Housing Trust, Fountain Court, Oxford Spires Business Park, Kidlington, Oxfordshire OX5 1NZ, tel 01865 854 000. The Anchor Housing Trust also run an information line charged at local rates, redirecting calls to the nearest regional office, tel 0345 758 595.

Building Societies Association, 3 Saville Row, London W1X 1AF, tel 0171 437 0655.

Carers National Association (Carers), 20-25 Glasshouse Yard, London EC1A 4JS, tel 0171 490 8898.

Cinnamon Trust, Foundry House, Foundry Square, Hayle TR27 4HH, tel 01736 757 900.

Energy Action Grants Agency, EAGA Ltd., Eldon Court, Eldon Square, Newcastle NE1 7HA, tel freephone 0800 181 667

Independent Housing Ombudsman, Norman House, 105-109 The Strand, London WC2R 0AA, tel 0171 836 3630.

Local Government Ombudsman (for England), 21 Queen Anne's Gate, London SW1H 9BU, tel 0171 915 3210, and (for Wales), Derwen House, Court Road, Bridgend CF31 1BN, tel 01656 661 325.

Royal Association for Disability and Rehabilitation (RADAR), 12 City Forum, 250 City Road, London EC1V 8AF, tel 0171 250 3222.

Shelter, 88 Old Street, London EC1V 9HU, tel 0171 505 2000. Information on all aspects of housing rights.

Work and Retirement

Advisory Conciliation and Arbitration Service (ACAS), Brandon House, 180 Borough High Street, London SE1 1LW, tel 0171 210 3000, and 3 Purbeck House, Lambourne Crescent, Llanishen, Cardiff, tel 01222 761 126.

Commission for Racial Equality, Elliott House,

10-12 Allington Street, London SW1E 5EH, tel 0171 828 7022. Information on the all aspects of the Race Relations Acts, including employment, housing, harassment and unfair discrimination.

Department for Education and Employment, Public Enquiries, Sanctuary Buildings, Great Smith Street, London SW1P 3BT, tel 0171 925 5555. Able to provide information and answer questions about aspects of the law in training and at work.

Department of Trade and Industry, Employment Relations, 1 Victoria Street, London SW1H 0ET, tel 0171 215 5000, can give information on employment protection rights.

Employment Rights Advice Service, run by the Low Pay Unit, 27-29 Amwell Street, London EC1R 1UN, tel 0171 713 7616. An Advice Line, tel 0171 713 7583. The Service can give information on all aspects of employment and benefit law.

Equal Opportunities Commission, Overseas House, Quay Street, Manchester M3 3HN; tel 0161 833 9244, and Caerwys House, Windsor Lane, Cardiff CF1 1LB, tel 01222 343 552. Enquiries can be made through the Information Section, open 9.30am-4.30pm, Mon-Fri.

Health and Safety Executive Information Centre, Public Enquiry Point, Broad Lane, Sheffield S3 7HQ. The Health and Safety Executive are responsible for checking on health and safety at work throughout England and Wales. They can send you leaflets and other information explaining the law and can tell you who to contact if you have a health and safety problem with training or work. They also run the HSE Infoline, tel 0541 545500, open Mon-Fri 8.30am-5.00pm.

Lesbian and Gay Employment Rights (LAGER), Unit 1g, Leroy House, 436 Essex Road, London N1 3QP, advising lesbians and gay men encountering discrimination at work

because of their sexuality, tel 0171 704 8066 (lesbian rights) and 0171 704 6066 (gay men).

REACH, Bear Wharf, 27 Bankside, London SE1 9ET, tel 0171 928 0452.

Stonewall, 16 Clerkenwell Close, London EC1R 0AA, tel 0171 336 8860, campaigns for equality for lesbians, gay men and bisexuals and able to provide information on these issues.

Money

Association of British Insurers, Consumer Information Dept., 51 Gresham Street, London EC2V 7HQ, tel 0171 600 3333, can provide leaflets and further information on insurance.

Banking Ombudsman, 70 Gray's Inn Road, London WC1X 8NB, tel 0171 404 9944.

Benefit Enquiry Line for People with Disabilities, open Mon-Fri 8.30am-6.30pm and Sat 9.00am-1.00pm, tel 0800 88 22 00.

Court of Protection, Stewart House, 24

Kingsway, London WC2B
6HD, tel 0171 664 7000.

Inland Revenue, Public
Enquiry Room, Room
G1A, West Wing,
Somerset House, The
Strand, London WC2R
1LB, tel 0171 438 7772.
Free leaflets and
information on taxation.
Inland Revenue Helpline
tel 0645 000 444, charged
at local rates. The service
operates Mon-Fri 5pm-
10pm and Sat-Sun 8am-
10pm, with a possiblity of
the weekday hours being
extended into the
morning and early
afternoon.

**Insurance Ombudsman
Bureau**, City Gate One,
135 Park Street, London
SE1 9EA, tel 0845 600 66
66 (low call).

**Occupational Pensions
Advisory Service**,
(OPAS) 11 Belgrave
Road, London. SW1V
1RB, tel 0171 233 8080.

Pensions Ombudsman,
11 Belgrave Road,
London SW1V 1RB, tel
0171 834 9144.

War Pensions Helpline,
open Mon-Thurs 8.15am-
5.15pm, Fri 8.15am -4.30
pm, tel 01253 858 858.

Travel and Transport

**Central Rail Users'
Committee**, 8 Duncannon
St., London WC2N 4JF,
tel 0171 505 9090.

**Department of
Environment, Transport
and the Regions Enquiry
Service** can provide
information on motoring
and transport law, tel
0171 271 4800, normal
office hours.

**Driving Standards
Agency**, Stanley House,
56 Talbot Street,
Nottingham NG1 5GU,
tel 0115 901 2516
(customer service and
enquiries).

DVLA (Driving and
Vehicle Licensing
Agency), Licensing
Centre, Swansea, SA6
7JL, for enquiries over
driving licences, tax discs
or a particular vehicle, tel
01792 772 151.

**London Regional
Passenger Committee**,
Clements House, 14-18
Gresham Street, London
EC2V 7PR, tel 0171
505 9000.

London Underground,

Customer Services, 55
Broadway London SW1H
0BD, tel 0171 918 4040.

Motor Insurers' Bureau,
152 Silbury Boulevard,
Milton Keynes MK9
1NB, tel 01908 240 000.

Rail Regulator, 1
Waterhouse Square, 138-
142 Holborn, London
EC1N 2ST, tel 0171
282 2000.

Goods and Services

Office of Fair Trading,
Field House, 15-25
Bream's Buildings,
London EC4A 1PR, tel
0171 211 8000. The
official watchdog,
protecting consumers'
interests. They can't give
advice on individual
cases, but can send
information on the law or
put you in touch with
someone who may be able
to help. They have a
Public Liaison Unit able
to deal with general
enquiries, who can be
contacted at cheap local
rates, tel 0345 22 44 99.

**Mail Order
Protection Scheme**, 16
Tooks Court, London
EC4A 1LB, tel 0171
405 6806.

Leisure

ABTA (The Association of British Travel Agents), 68-71 Newman Street, London W1P 4HQ, have an information line dealing with general advice on ABTA, its members and other travel information, tel 0891 202 520 (calls charged at 50p per minute) all other enquiries, tel 0171 637 2444.

BBC Radio, Broadcasting House, Portland Place, London W1A 1AA, tel 0171 580 4468.

BBC Television, Television Centre, Wood Lane, London W12 7RJ, tel 0181 743 8000.

British Canoe Union, Adbolton Lane, West Bridgford, Nottingham NG2 5AS, tel 0115 982 1100.

Broadcasting Standards Agency, Stanley House, Talbot Street, Nottingham NG1 5GU, tel 01159 474 222.

Countryside Commission, John Dower House, Crescent Place, Cheltenham, Gloucestershire GL50 3RA, tel 01242 521381,

able to provide information on access and rights of way issues.

Environment Agency, Rio House, Waterside Drive, Aztec West, Almondsbury, Bristol BS12 4UD, tel 01454 624 400, run a free 24 hour phone line on which the public are asked to report any environmental incident, tel 0800 80 70 60.

Independent Television Commission, 33 Foley Street, London W1P 7LB, tel 0171 255 3000.

National Benevolent Fund for the Aged, 1 Leslie Grove Place, Croyden, Surrey, tel 0181 688 6655.

Open College of the Arts, Houndhill, Worsbrough, Barnsley, South Yorkshire S70 6TU, tel 01226 730 495.

Open University, Walton Hall, Milton Keynes, MK7 6AA, tel 01908 274 066.

Royal Society for the Prevention of Cruelty to Animals (RSPCA) have a 24 hour emergency line on which people can report an animal in distress, tel 0990 555 999. For information or advice

contact The RSPCA Public Enquiry Section, Causeway, Horsham, West Sussex, RH12 1HG, tel 01403 264 181.

Women's Institute, The National Federation of Women's Institutes, 104 New Kings Roadd, London SW6 4LY, tel 0171 371 9300.

Workers' Education Association, 17 Victoria Park Square, London E2 9PB, tel 0181 983 1515.

Safety

Criminal Injuries Compensation Authority, Tay House, 300 Bath Street, Glasgow, G2 4JR, tel 0141 331 2726.

Rape Crisis Centres, are located throughout Britain offering to free and confidential advice to any woman or girl who has been raped or sexually assaulted. Contact Directory Enquiries or tel 0171 837 1600.

Survivors, PO Box 2470, London SW9 9ZP tel 0171 833 3737. Helpline open Mon & Tues, 7pm-10pm giving advice and information for men who have suffered sexual vio-

CONTACTS

lence as children or adults.

Suzy Lamplugh Trust, 14
East Sheen Avenue,
London SW14 8AS, tel
0181 392 1839. Practical
information, guidance
and resources on personal
safety in all situations.

Victim Support, Cranmer
House, 39 Brixton Road,
London SW9 6DZ, tel
0171 735 9166. Offers
emotional support,
information and practical
help to victims of crime.
Victim support also run a
helpline, providing support
to people who have been
victims of crime, Mon-Fri
9am-9pm; Sat-Sun 9am-
7pm, tel 0845 30 30 900
(local rates).

The Legal System

Law Centres Federation,
Duchess House, 18-19
Warren Street, London
W1P 5DB, tel 0171 387
8570, can give you the
name and address of your
nearest law centre.

Legal Aid Board, head
office, 85 Grays Inn Road,
London WC1X 8AA, tel
0171 813 1000.
Information leaflets
available on applying for
legal aid. To find a Legal
Aid franchised firm in

your area, call free on
0500 282 300

**Legal Services
Ombudsman**, 22 Oxford
Court, Oxford Street,
Manchester M2 3WQ, tel
0161 236 9532.

**Office for the
Supervision of Solicitors**,
Victoria Ct., 8 Dormer
Place, Leamington Spa,
Warwickshire, CV32
5AE, tel 01926 820 082,
deal with complaints from
the public about the
service they have received
from a solicitor.

**Police Complaints
Authority**, 10 Great
George Street, London
SW1P 3AE, tel 0171 273
6450. The official body
established to oversee
complaints against the
police, which can provide
information on how to
make a complaint if you
have witnessed or suffered
police misconduct.

Government

European Commission, 8
Storey's Gate,
Westminster, London
SW1P 3AT, tel 0171 973
1992. Leaflets available.
If you 'phone, ask for the
Information Section.
European Parliament

Information Office, 2
Queen Anne's Gate,
London SW1H 9AA, tel
0171 227 4300. An
information service on all
matters relating to the
European Parliament.
There is a library open
Tues, Wed, Thurs, 10-1 &
2-5, but before you go
ring to check if they have
the information you want.

**Local Government
Ombudsman**,
Commission for Local
Administration in
England, 21 Queen
Anne's Gate, London
SW1H 9BU, tel 0171 915
3210, also Derwen House,
Court Road, Brigend, Mid
Glamorgan CF31 1BN,
tel 01656 661325.

**Parliamentary
Ombudsman**,
Parliamentary
Commissioner for
Administration, Church
House, Great Smith
Street, London SW1P
3BW, tel 0171 276 2130.

**Public Information
Office**, House of
Commons, 1 Derby Gate,
London SW1A 2DG, tel
0171 219 4272. A public
information service on
matters to do with the
working and proceedings
of Parliament.

A

Access to
information 15, 182
Adoption 29
Air travel 138
Alcohol - drinking
and driving 106-8,
- licensing laws 126
Allotments 136
Animals
- dogs 132-3
- pet 132-3
- wild 135
Assault
- & battery 144-5
- domestic violence
148
- indecent 148-9

B

Bail 162
Banks 87
Beaches 134
Benefits
- Attendance
Allowance 82
- Council Tax 85
- Disabled Living
Allowance 81, 100
- Disability Working
Allowance 81
- Funeral Payment
33
- Housing Benefit 84
- Incapacity Benefit
80
- Income Support 83
- Jobseeker's
Allowance 80
- Social Fund 83-4
Bigamy 22
Boating 135
Bulls 135
Burglary 144
Buses
- complaints over
services 96
- fares & tickets 96,
98

C

Carers 51, 82
Charter Mark 182
Charters
- Benefits Agency 83
- Citizen's 182
- Community Care
52
- Council Tenant's 42
- Court user's 151,
164
- Jobseeker's 69
- Passenger's 96, 97
- Patient's 9, 14, 17
- Redundancy
Payments Service
69
- Taxpayer's 91
- Traveller's 139
- Victim's 150-1
Chiropodists 8
Citizen's arrest 146
Coach travel 98, 99
Community care 50-2
Compensation
- criminal injuries
150-2
- ruined holiday 138,
141
- road accidents
104, 105
Consumer law 108-
9, 114-24, 127, 137-8
Contract
- consumer 96, 97,
116-7, 129, 137-8
- at work 62-3
- unfair 116
Court
- of Appeal 166, 175
- county 166
- Crown 165-6
- European Court of
Justice 176
- High 167
- magistrates' 167
- of Protection 88-9
- small claims
procedure 120

- system of
precedent 175
- youth 167
Crash helmets 105
Credit 122, 124
Credit cards 115,
122-3, 138
Criminal Injuries
Compensation
Authority 150-2
Criminal
responsibilty 161-2
Crown Prosecution
Service 161, 166
Customs 139
Cycling 112

D

Death 30-8, 142
Dentists 6-7
Discrimination
- at work 58-61
- disability 61, 100,
121
- racial 58, 60, 121
- sex 59-60, 98-9,
121
- sexuality 59
Divorce 25-29
- care of children
26-8
- grandparents 28-9
- separation 25
Doctors
- changing or finding
5
- complaint against a
17-20
- confidentially 15,
16, 101
Dogs 132-3
Driving
- age 101
- careless 106-7
- dangerous 106-7
- drunken 106-8
- licence 101
Duty solicitor 159-
60, 162

E

Education 72
Elections 177-81
Electoral Register
177-9
Enduring power of
attorney 87-8
Engagements 23
European
- Convention on
Human Rights 176-7
- Court 99
- Commission 176
- Council of
Ministers 176
- elections 180-1
- Parliament 176,
180-1
Eviction 47

F

Fingerprints 160
Fishing 135-6
Footpaths 134
Funerals 32-4

G

Gambling 128
Grandparents 28-9
Guarantees 115, 119

H

Harassment 146-7
- by landlord 47
- racial 146
- sexual 60
Hire purchase 123
Holidays 137-142
Home
- improvement
grants 40-1
- moving 52-6
- property rights 24
- residential &
nursing 53
- security 152-4
Hospitals
- complaints 17-20
- leaving 12-3
- treatment 9